"Free Parking is classically contrarian, flying in the face of every bit of self-serving wisdom to today's vendors of mutual funds, banking products and insurance dispense about retirement in Canada."—— Jonathan Chevreau *The National Post*

"Alan Dickson is living large on less. And how he does it has repercussions and perhaps hope for all those would - be early retirees, rat race runners and toxic-job holders who dream of finding a way out"——Tony Wanless *Vancouver Province*

"His views provoke controversy as they go beyond the accepted wisdom of financial management" ——Gil Parker, *Victoria Times Colonist*

"Alan Dickson measures riches in terms of leisure time spent with family and friends. He'd like to help you do the same." ——David Pyette, *The Globe and Mail*

"I think it should be compulsory reading for the twenty somethings and newlyweds..thanks for the very good book."——Ross Butterfield, Victoria senior

Free Parking

Free Parking

A 2nd Look at Financial Planning

Alan Dickson

National Library of Canada Cataloguing in Publication Data

Dickson, Alan, 1951 -
    Free Parking : a 2nd look at financial planning

Includes bibliographical references.
ISBN 0-9688855-0-0

    1. Finance, Personal.   2. Investments.   3. Financial security.
I. Title

HG179.D52 2001   332.024'01   C2001-900635-7

First Printing June 2001
Second Printing August 2001

Published by:
Preferred Marketing Inc.
www.freemoneypress.com

Printed in Canada

Dedicated to

Mom: who taught me to play Monopoly, ask questions and listen to my mother.

My Wife, Debra: the personification of patience as I struggle with answers to the questions.

My Daughter, Rachel: who constantly reminds me to talk to my wife and listen to my mother.

Thank You

To the Rich and Prosperous who have made Canada their home. To the highly paid captains of industry and government alike; with their seven figure salaries, bonuses and severance packages. To all those toiling to advance their social and economic status, determined to climb into the upper-income brackets. To the myriads of investment advisors and their devoted clients who have amassed hundreds of millions in RRSPs — all to be taxed at a future date: you have my profound thank-you.

I go to bed content each night in the knowledge that your dedication and generous contributions to our tax system have secured my future benefits.

Table of Contents

Preface 8

1. Perception — or is that deception 13

2. Financial Freedom — who wants to be a millionaire?. . . 17

3. Career Choices — be careful what you wish for 34

4. Possessions — say goodbye to the Joneses 67

5. Financial Fables — part 1 Investments 88

6. Financial Fables — part 2 Insurance 110

7. Financial Planners — who are these people? 134

8. Taxes — a nice source of income 141

9. Retirement please — and hold the taxes 158

10. Estate planning — a dying business 175

The Last Word 181

About the Author 183

PREFACE

Before computers there was Monopoly. Before video games there was Monopoly. Before vcr's, dvd's, and cd's there was Monopoly.

On a long winter evening a family gathers around the table close to the kitchen wood stove and learn the facts of life. They learn about real estate. "One-two-three-four...Marvin Gardens. I'll buy it! Here's my three hundred." They learn about making the deal. "I'll trade you two railroads for Atlantic. They're worth more but you need help. Come on, take it or leave it." They learn about taxes. "Forty dollars per house! I'm ruined, I'll have to take off half my houses. It's not fair." They learn about bankruptcy. "Hotel on Marvin Gardens, twelve hundred dollars. That's it, I'm broke."

I learn about *FREE PARKING*. As the game intensifies and life gets more hazardous; with hotels on New York, Tennessee and St. James and houses on all the reds, I seek temporary asylum by landing on Free Parking. Years later with the desire for quick money, the rules have changed in my household. Taxes are gathered and placed in the centre of the board to be won by the one landing on Free Parking. No longer just a place of refuge and reflection, it is now a integral part of winning; an observation not lost on one seeking an analogy of life.

While most purveyors of financial planning and investment advice are focusing on the accumulation of money and properties, I heartily recommend that you spend some time on Free Parking. Step aside from the wheeling and dealing, the buying and selling, the casting of the die to advance your position. Occasionally it is beneficial to be a thoughtful observer rather than a player. I know that this is not conventional wisdom. We are continually shown the beautiful people of the world; you know the ones, the rich and famous. I've just finished reading an article about another twenty-something year old who's made it on the Forbes list of the rich and influential business leaders. Great, I'll add him to *my* list of kids whose sole purpose is to expose me as a failure. Sorry, I believe the universally accepted word for that feeling is Loser. My list includes my 32 year old doctor who wants to look at my 49 year old prostate. Then there's my 26 year old banker. She wants to see if I still qualify for my 30 year old mortgage.

But it's not just these young upstarts who bother me. These new gurus who are telling me the rules of living and the definition of success. It's my peers as well; we've all been seduced into measuring success within the most narrow of parameters. Is success a celebrity status accompanied by riches and power? Or could it be defined in the faces of an elderly couple? Study them as they sit on a park bench holding hands, reflecting on the past with words un-uttered. Their bodies reveal the passage of time and life with all its scrapes and scars. But in their eyes you behold the satisfaction of a job well done and a commitment to a life of loving and sharing that embraces not just two but family and community.

So there you have it. The reason behind the writing of this book. It's about looking at our priorities and re-examining the definition of success. It will show you how to make wise insurance and investment decisions for yourself without being sold the latest commission driven product. You'll learn of the extra cash that you can put in your pocket courtesy of the provincial and federal government. Mostly it's about money. No. No more advice promoting dollar cost averaging mutual funds. You've read enough about the ten percent solution to prosperity, the no-pain-no-gain philosophy or even how to pick a winning lottery ticket. Think about Free Parking. Look at what you have now. Is it possible that the new job or promotion that seems so important will be a step backwards? Why are you knocking yourself out to have all that money in a retirement savings plan? Do the middle class really have more fun than those living below the poverty line?

We are introduced to several people, who share with us life experiences, that have molded their views on ambition, investments, and retirement. Yet, we already know them. You may not know them as Walter and Mary, but you've seen them working in their beautiful yards on picturesque settings, and asked "why not me?" You may not recognize them as Adam and Nancy, but you've seen him merrily go about his 'menial' occupation, and wondered what makes him happier than those with 'better' jobs. And you've watched the Tims and Sandys of this world enjoying time with their children, at an hour when 'normal' parents are preoccupied with work; while their children reveal their innermost thoughts to strangers at care centres.

This is not about giving up and being cared for by the state. We don't need any more politicians! This is about making choices and thriving. It's about vacationing in the most beautiful places in the world; dining on the choicest of food. It's about living like the well- to- do only doing it better.

Enjoy!

Alan Dickson
Duncan, B.C.
December 2000

1

PERCEPTION:
OR IS THAT
DECEPTION?

"Oh what a tangled web
we weave, when first we
practice to deceive." — Shakespeare

I have a confession to make. When designing the cover of *Free Parking*, I had an idea that I thought would illustrate the problem that I believe exists with popular financial planning advice. I would solicit comments about the book from Bill Gates, Paul Martin and Stephen King. I even called them. They may be still waiting for me to send a draft copy to read. I was prepared to write suitable 'praise' for *Free Parking*. Bill Gates would say: "So this is the way Monopoly is played. I wish someone would tell the justice department." Paul Martin would add: "Finally someone understands the beauty of a budget." And Stephen King would pen: "*Free Parking* explains why RRSPs are scarier than anything I have created!"

That's right I called them all. Bill Gates lives in Port Alberni. Paul Martin is in Victoria and Stephen King comes from Sooke.

Of course they're not *the Bill Gates* and company. But you

could be momentarily deceived into believing that these celebrities had endorsed this book. My wife said it was a dumb idea. She's usually right. But it would have been fun to see the reaction. And it's not an original idea.

This book is about perception...and deception. Sometimes we are deceived by others. I hope you recognize them in their roles played here. Sometimes we are self-deceived. We want to believe, even when every neuron in our brain cries out "BEWARE!" The reality is, that the celebrity names that you may have thought and hoped had endorsed this product would find little to interest them in this book. Not unlike the rich and famous who actually lend their names to products we buy everyday. We think because a sports star has his name on these running shoes, it will make us a better athlete when we buy them. We think because a movie star has her name on this lipstick we will be more beautiful when we wear it. We think because a wealthy tycoon endorses this financial product we will be rich if we buy it. Are we really so naive as to believe this? Perhaps. But maybe we just want to follow. After all, if we're a follower, when things go wrong we don't need to take responsibility. We just blame our leader. Our only decision is to choose whom we will follow. We are drawn to luminaries in the business and entertainment world. We know that countless others are following them and we seek safety in numbers.

Free Parking is really about challenging the financial experts. This book will question everything that you have been told about financial planing. It has been conceived to show you how to think for yourself and to ask the question: Why? Why is this financial expert telling me this? Is he just repeating what he has been trained to say or do the facts support the statements? We all like to believe that we are individuals and we think for ourselves, but nothing could be farther from the truth. Do you know of anyone who truly does? If you do, commend him or her the next time you meet. She is a rarity. Especially in the field of finance. Someone makes a guess about the next week's performance of the stock market. If he guesses correctly, he becomes a guru to be revered and watched for the next decade. If he should say that he no longer fancies a particular stock, the market, like a fickle child in a sea of toys, drops the stock and runs to pick up the next. Often the stock sheds hundreds of millions, perhaps billions of dollars in market capitalization. Yet, what has changed from the day before? Perhaps there have been some disappointments in earnings or a change of personnel, but these items should have been already factored into the price. No, for the most part, the fund managers and investment gurus that we idolize and blindly turn our decisions over to, will sell their prized stock in a heartbeat because everybody else has. And you want to trust them with your future!

We listen to the "experts" that insist we must begin now to save for our retirement or risk spending our golden years in a cold apartment eating cat food. But where is the evidence? In the past twenty years, has there ever been an elderly person in Canada subjected to this standard of living? Occasionally, yes. There are unique situations when this occurs, but is it the norm? In British Columbia, the poorest of seniors who are Canadian citizens and have lived in Canada for at least ten years are guaranteed an income that will keep them warm, dry, and well fed. Some may choose to spend this income on items other than food and housing. This is a matter of choice. Almost twenty years ago, a neighbour died of exposure in his unheated house. He had been living in the basement. The roof had large holes in it. He had refused any help to have it repaired. When he had not ventured out for several days the RCMP were called and his body was discovered. Thousands of dollars stuffed inside of jars were also discovered. He had made a choice. You may argue that the social programs that surround us are eroding and therefore we must take action to replace them with private funds. But where is the evidence? For all the hue and cry (mostly from politicians or special interest groups), Canada's safety net is not becoming unraveled. A careful study will show that there are more programs available for seniors than at any other time in Canada's history.

Free Parking has not been written to give you another expert to follow. I want to prod you into thinking for yourself. When we stop listening to the experts and start thinking for ourselves we regain control of our life. We are no longer living under a cloud of despair and uncertainty because we have not acquired some prescribed minimum in our RRSPs or investment account. We can begin enjoying life now rather than assigning such enjoyment as a future reward only for those who have made suitable sacrifices to some 'God of Riches.'

2

FINANCIAL FREEDOM:
WHO WANTS TO BE
A MILLIONAIRE?

"Money doesn't necessarily have any
connection with happiness. Maybe with
unhappiness." — Industrialist J. Paul Getty

I never liked owning Boardwalk and Park Place. When our family played Monopoly my siblings aspired to greatness. They would gloat about owning these showy properties. I couldn't wait to get rid of them! These bastions of the upper crust surrounded by taxes: luxury tax, income tax and community chess with the dreaded house assessment.

They were high maintenance. Seven hundred and fifty dollars to buy the property and two hundred dollars for every house. The odds of someone landing on your establishment were against you. Only two chances per round while most other groups were in threes. Indeed many entire games were played while the hapless proprietor of Boardwalk and Park Place sat in despair watching would be patrons speed by advancing to Go. In the unlikely event that someone did land on Boardwalk with a hotel on it, it was overkill. You hardly needed to charge $2,000 to vanquish your opponent. I just didn't understand the lure of the super-rich. Give me Virginia, States and St.Charles in the low rental district next to the jail and my beloved Free Parking. My family thought I would grow out of this aversion to excess. It's not that I dislike the good things in life. On the contrary, there are many wonderful experiences and possessions that I have and will have in the future. However, I do resist the excessive price that is so often attached to these good things. Many look at the price and do one of two things: Some dismiss the thought of ever enjoying these and allow this to mar their outlook on life and the future. Others become obsessed with acquiring the good life at any cost, and sacrifice the present for the future. We'll discuss these attitudes later. Suffice for now is the realization that the concern about our future enjoyment and well-being has resulted in a bonanza for magazines and books dedicated to creating the State of Financial Utopia. An ever increasing horde of financial planners are eager to book us passage on the good ship SS Mutualfund.

In Monopoly it's pretty easy to pick out the winner when the game is over. He's the one left with all the money and properties. How do you pick out the winner in life? Some say, "He who dies with the most toys wins." That attitude hardly deserves a comment. Many speak of financial freedom as a mark of success. Would you agree?   If you do then you are in good company. But how would you describe financial freedom? Perhaps it's like a postcard that you received several years ago— a picture of a tropical island. You've been carrying it in the pocket of your favourite jeans all this time. It's well worn and you send it through the wash on occasion. Today the wind is cold, the first sign of another long winter, and you instinctively pull out the postcard to have another look at "your" island. You can still make out the outline of some palm trees but you can't exactly recall all the details. Nevertheless you still agree with the heading:"Wish You Were Here!" But where is 'here'? Is there some way to enhance the clarity of this postcard so we know where we want to go and why we are making all of these plans?

Many find themselves with endless questions when they begin to think about organizing their finances with an uncertain future ahead of them. Tim Andrew was one of these. However, Tim had the advantage of a conversation with Walter Sanderson—a man who Tim respected and admired. Listen as Tim explains what took place that changed his thinking.

"I've made arrangements to talk with Walter Sanderson. Everyone says Walter's rich. So he should be able to help me with my financial planning. I'm sure he can get my plan a little more in focus so I know where I'm going. I met Walter when I came to Vancouver Island ten years ago. I think he was already retired. He and his wife Mary live in a beautiful Tudor-style house in Oak Bay, high above the beach overlooking the Straight of Georgia. They live quietly behind the pyramid cedar hedges that offer their owners the blessing of obscurity. I've talked to Walter in the yard a few times over the years. He's always in the yard; shaping the hedges, mowing lawns, tending the flowers—beautiful rhododendrons, irises, roses and countless other flowering shrubs and plants. My wife and I often remarked about the paradise that surrounds the Sanderson estate. The wildlife enjoy their generosity and repay them with their presence, adding to the wonder of the place. We always marvel at how the deer and rabbits eat the provisions left for them but leave the shrubs. Have they made a personal agreement with their hosts? It must have been a marvelous place to raise a family. We have only met two of their four children.. The youngest was still home when we first arrived, but soon she had followed the others, no doubt to some idyllic life of pleasure. Such is the lot of those who have achieved financial freedom. It appears to percolate through generations bestowing an aura upon them of security and contentment.

"The grand old house, built by a lumber baron, must seem so empty now with just the two of them. They do have guests. Two or three times a year people come. Walter fires up the Lincoln and picks them up at the airport. They keep a guest cottage ready. Once Mary had seen us walking by and we were invited into the cottage for a cup of tea. She must have been getting it ready for visitors. It looked so inviting that a couple could live their forever. In the fall, when the lawns have been mowed for the last time, the last of the apples have been gathered and the roses have been tucked into bed until spring, the Sandersons go away for several weeks. My wife and I fantasize about what exotic locale they are touring while we pick up their newspapers and check the perimeter of the house to make sure it is secure. This year we are going to ask about their travels.

"'Well Tim, have you been waiting long?'

"'Oh! Hi Walter, I guess you caught me daydreaming or

talking to myself. I'm not sure which. Thanks for coming. When I spoke with you on the phone about financial planning I didn't think that you'd be offering to meet with me so soon. But I'm sure glad that you could.'

"'I'm curious about this whole evolution of financial planning. Time was, if you needed a savings or chequing account you went down to the local bank; if you wanted to buy or sell stocks you had an account with a stockbroker, and if you wanted life insurance... well, you didn't have to go anywhere a life insurance salesman would find you soon enough! Now they're all calling themselves 'financial planners'.You even have lawyers and accountants getting into the mix. Around RRSP time everyone from your barber to the kid at the 7-Eleven is talking about their financial plan.'

"'You mean, Walter, you and your wife don't have a financial plan?'

"'Oh we have a plan alright. But it might not be quite what you have in mind.'

"'Well it's sure worked for you. Could you fill me in on some of the details of your plan?'

"'Sure; but first tell me about your plan. What do you want this plan to accomplish for you?'

"'Two words, Walter: FINANCIAL FREEDOM!'

"'And what do you see for your future when you say financial freedom?'

"'I see long vacations on tropical islands. I see reliving history in Europe. I see new cars—new German cars. I see designer clothes and five star resorts and restaurants. I see not having to check prices when I shop. I see security and happiness for my family. I see a beautiful house on oceanfront property—like yours, Walter.'

"'Boy you sure see a lot and in a hurry. You must have that list written down somewhere.'

"'It's on my fridge. One of the books on financial planning said you should keep your goals visible. You can't get much more visible than a fridge. It's already helped my wife attain one of her goals. I bought her a bigger fridge.'

"'How much money will you need to meet all of these goals?'

"'Well, I've read the books and made out our plan. Allowing for inflation it comes to just over one million. I know it sounds like a lot but I've got thirty years until I want to retire. Time is on my side.....'

"Walter quickly interjected. 'Let me guess, you read that in one of the books! Tell me, Tim, do you think anyone else has these same goals?'

"'Oh sure; all my friends want to be financially free. You should see my brother-in-law's fridge! And the guys at work, they've all read the books.'

"'Have any of them reached this goal of financial freedom?'

"'Are you kidding? We only started last month!'

"'What about some older friends or relatives? Are any of them financially free, using your measurements?'

"'There's my Uncle Heber in Arizona. My mom always said that he was loaded, but I'm not sure what she actually meant because I never met him.'

"'Have you ever met a millionaire?'

"'I've got autographs of most of the Vancouver Canucks. I'll bet they're all millionaires.'

"'No doubt many of them earn well over a million dollars. But they may not wind up as millionaires, and they certainly don't represent your average millionaire. Would you like to meet an average millionaire?'

"'Oh, would I ever!'

"'Let's go across the street to the restaurant and I'll introduce you if you want.'

"'That's a good one, Walter. You're going to pick out a millionaire in Swiss Chalet! If I had that kind of money do you think you'd find me in a Swiss Chalet? I mean where's the imported delicacies and vintage wines?'

"'I'm not sure about the wine list but there's good quality and low prices. That's important to most millionaires.'

"'They care about prices?'

"'Just like you and me. There's a good crowd today—over a hundred customers. Now, according to statistics three of them should be millionaires.'

"'Really! That many? Canadians are richer than I thought.'

"'That's a North American average. About three per cent of the households have a net worth of at least one million dollars. Do you think you can spot any millionaires in here?'

"'Look, Walter! Heading for the door! The guy with the gold watch and the chains. That Armani suit must have set him back $1500. He's our man. Look at the young lady he's wearing on his arm. She's half his age. You've gotta have a million bucks to live like that!'

"'Well, you're half right.'

"'How can I be half right? Is he a millionaire or not?'

"'Yes, he is. At least for now. He earned his money the old fashioned way. When he turned twenty-one his daddy gave him a million. He's been back twice for more. I don't think you can learn much about financial independence from that millionaire. Unless you've got a rich relative who's very fond of you, I think we have to look elsewhere for a mentor.'

"'Well, I can't see any other likely candidates. Let's go down to the yacht club.'

"'Most millionaires don't hang out at yacht clubs.'

"'Who do?'

"'People who want to look like millionaires and people who are looking for millionaires. Let's look a little more right here. I'll give you some help. You see that elderly gentleman in the grey cardigan sitting by himself.'

"'Nooo!!' The words drooled out of my mouth in disbelief.

"'That's old Mr. Carl Jackson, and he's your bonafide millionaire. That younger man that you spotted, with his even younger wife, was Carl Junior. They were sitting at the same table but you can lay odds that they were not here to eat. They dropped in to see Daddy, probably needing a little cash.'

"'What's Mr. Jackson in here for?'

"'Probably the quarter chicken special. He eats here fairly regularly since his wife went into the hospital. He comes here after visiting hours.'

"'How did Mr. Jackson make his money?'

"'He worked hard.'

"'I can do that.'

"'He saved every spare nickel.'

"'Uh...I could do that.. I guess. For how long?'

"'He never stopped. He is still saving. He doesn't enjoy spending money. His only extravagance is giving money to his son. And he's not happy about that but he told me that he's paying for a mistake he made years ago.'

"'What kind of mistake?'

"'He took his son with him one day when he went to see his lawyer. The lawyer told young Carl that he should be proud of his dad. 'You're a lucky young fellow, your dad is a wealthy man.' Ever since then Junior's been trying to spend it. Mr. Jackson thought that by giving his son a million dollars when he turned twenty-one Carl would be motivated to invest it in a business and make something of himself, but it only made matters worse. It just confirmed what the lawyer had said: Mr. Jackson was a wealthy man. Carl couldn't see any reason to go into business, or for that matter do anything to earn money. Dad had all the money that he would need.'

"'But, surely Carl must have known that his parents were wealthy before the lawyer said anything. What about their house or the cars?'

"'The Jackson's live in the same house they bought before Carl was born. A modest storey and half across the river. Carl lives in a penthouse condominium on the inner harbour. As for cars, Mr. Jackson drives a five year old Pontiac. His son just left in his new Porsche.'

"'And here comes millionaire number three!'

"'I hope he's easier to spot than Mr. Jackson. I still can't believe that someone with all that money wouldn't want to spend some of it.'

"'Then he wouldn't have 'all that money' would he? Now have a good look around for our new man and see if you can identify him.'

"'Give me a hint, Walter. Can I tell by the clothes? Is his wife here?'

"'Yes to both of your questions. You can tell by his clothes. He's wearing an apron. And his wife is here, but I bet she's in the kitchen.'

"'That old guy bussing tables is a millionaire! What's he doing working here?'

"'He's doing what all dedicated business owners do. He's minding his own business. Mr. Chan took over this franchise twelve years ago when many his age would have been slowing down. He was already well off but he was ready for another business. He sure picked a demanding one. He's here seven days a week. His wife is here almost everyday. I guess that's the only way she would ever see him.'

"'Why does he do it?'

"'I guess he's happy working, watching his business grow. I can't give you a convincing reason because it's not my financial plan. It's Mr. Chan's.'

"'I don't want it to be my plan either! I gotta tell you, Walter, I'm pretty disappointed in this selection of millionaires. They sure aren't what I was expecting . They don't fit my vision of enjoying the good life. The only one that had some of the things on my list was chained to his father. He might have money to spend, but he sure doesn't have freedom! Walter, I know you said you would introduce me to Mr. Jackson and Mr. Chan, but I think I'd like to pass on that for now. I just can't see myself having too much in common with these gentlemen—I mean working and saving to end up spending my golden years like they are.'

"'I'll let you in on a little secret, Tim. I knew these two would be here. Carl Junior was a bonus. I thought you might see having wealth in a little different light. You see, what's made Mr. Jackson and Mr. Chan millionaires isn't some off- the- shelf- fill- in- the- blanks financial plan. It's who they are. They thrive on work and saving. Work and being frugal is not a means to reaching their goal it IS their goal. For someone else to adopt their way of life without having their propensity for work and saving would be anything but freedom.'

"'Are all the wealthy like that?'

"'It's like that lawyer joke: Not all lawyers are crooks: it's the 99% that give the rest a bad name! Not all of the country's millionaires are frugal penny pinchers, but many are. It stands to reason that if you have a natural desire to work hard and save money, you have a decent chance of accumulating a lot of money. But it is just as reasonable that you will not stop being this way as soon as you have reached some magic dollar figure. It would be just as difficult for Mr. Jackson to start to enjoy spending his money as it would be for his son to stop spending it. I don't think either of those events are likely to occur, do you?'

"'Maybe I should scrap the whole idea of financial planning. I know I'm not cut out to be like Mr. Jackson or Mr. Chan.'

"'Don't be too quick to quit. You've just added another piece of information to your plan. Let's see how that can be made to work for you. You don't want to be like Mr. Jackson and Mr. Chan. You have discovered that many wealthy individuals live like Mr. Jackson and Mr. Chan. Before you draw any conclusions let me ask you: Why did you feel the need to become a millionaire?'

"'To have all the things I listed off to you earlier. You know the car, the clothes.....'

"'The freedom.'

"'Yes, mostly the freedom!'

"'Tell me; how many people were in the restaurant?'

"'You said about 100.'

"'And we examined 3. As for the other 97, did they look sadder or happier than the three we looked at?'

"'I didn't notice. I couldn't tell the millionaires from the rest, remember. Except for Carl Jackson and I didn't see him laughing.'

"'I didn't see much difference either. Their happiness didn't have much to do with their bank account. It would be a pretty sad world if you have to be a millionaire to be happy because the reality is that most of us will not acquire that kind of wealth in our lifetime.'

"'But I read that the number of wealthy individuals is growing as never before.'

"'Yes, and the number of the poor is growing as never before.'

"'How can that be, Walter? Can both classes be growing at the same time?'

"'Sure, let me explain. Say in Canada we have 8,000,000 households. 3% or 240,000 of those households are millionaires. Our population grows by 1% and next year we have 80,000 more households. What if our millionaire households grow by twice as fast as the population? Pretty impressive stuff that politicians—at least those on the government side—will point to as a sign of a healthy economy and wonderful management. Our millionaire population is now at 245,000, a 5,000 household increase or 2% of 240,000. But we have an increase of 80,000 households. That means that 75,000 didn't make it into the upper echelon of society. Some will become the middle class but you can be sure many, if not most, will be in the lower economic level.

"'Consider something else. When I was a boy, if you were a millionaire you had the world by the tail. You could go anywhere, do anything, live anywhere. Not anymore. There are many homes right here on Vancouver Island that are financially out of reach of a mere millionaire. With the spiraling cost of real estate and manpower, money has lost it's purchasing power.'

"'But that's my point, Walter. With inflation I'm going to

need that money just to buy the minimum to ensure a comfortable retirement.'

"'That depends how you describe a comfortable retirement and how you go about securing it. Just because some houses are beyond the reach of most of us, that shouldn't preclude us from owning a home if that's our desire. Let's turn your focus away from a bank account at your retirement and toward goals like making a contribution to family happiness and making a difference to people around you. You might find these more achievable and much more enjoyable to work towards. It's pretty hard to go fishing with a safety deposit box or go to watch a ball game with your RRSP.

"'But before you get to retirement, Tim, you've got a lot of living to do. Can you reach this million dollar level on your present savings plan, or do you need to count on higher earnings?'

"'Oh, of course, I'll need to be saving more than I do now. I'm putting aside 10% of my earnings. As my salary increases I'll still put aside 10% of my earnings, but it'll naturally be more; and, since I'll have more money, it'll be easier than it is now. I'm counting on my salary doubling every five years. I'm really starting to get noticed at Barton Brothers Department Store. Mr. Barton says I'm on the fast track to success. I've only been selling clothes for a year and a half but I've learned a lot. Mr. Barton says I have an eye for fashion. Did you notice how I spotted Carl Jackson's suit right off?'

"'Yes, Tim, I did notice that. I'm glad you like your job and

Mr. Barton notice's your work. It's nice to be appreciated. I know someone who worked at Barton Brothers a few years back. In fact he was in your department. He and his wife are in town for the weekend and they're staying with us. Why don't you and Sandy come over and meet them. His name is Adam Rarrie. Maybe he can give you some insight into your work.'

"'That would be great! He must know Gerry. He's been there for years. I'm always looking for someone with more experience that I can learn from—which is why I want to find out about your plan, Walter. Remember, you were going to fill me in on some of the details.'

"'If we have time Sunday after you and Adam finish talking shop I'll give you all the details. It's too late to get into it today. Besides, it would be good for our wives to be in on it. Mary's great for filling in when my mind omits a few details. In the meantime, think about the millionaires that we saw today and what we talked about. Tell Sandy that Mary will call her about this Sunday. See you then.' And Walter was gone, leaving me to resume talking to myself.

" Well, I don't know about you, but I have more questions than when I started. I know that I don't want to be another Mr. Chan or Mr. Jackson—not even Carl Jackson. But does that mean I don't want to be a millionaire at retirement? I'm going to write down some questions for Walter.

"**1**. If I don't focus on making and saving money for the future, how will I be able to retire? I'm only looking to be comfortable, but isn't that going to cost money?

"**2**. All the experts are saying the Canada Pension Plan will be broke before I retire. Isn't everyone going to be on his own, having to provide for himself?

"**3**. I know only 3 out of 100 have reached the level of assets that I feel I need to retire, but does that mean it's out of reach for me? After all, did anyone know about saving 10% of your income and financial planning thirty years ago? Won't many more be retiring wealthy with the economy as strong as it is and all the investing in mutual funds?

"**4**. If you didn't save every nickel, Walter, how can you afford to live in your beautiful house? The property taxes must be half what I earn!

"I'll have to watch how I word that last one. I don't want Walter to think that I feel he's hypocritical. Sandy will know best how to say that. I'm going home to tell her about my conversation with Walter, as well as, the invitation. We've been wanting to see inside Walter and Mary's house for years. Sandy will be thrilled.

"I didn't get to surprise Sandy with the invitation to the Sandersons. Mary had already called, and I was the one in for a surprise.

"'Walter didn't say anything about supper. I thought we were just going over for the afternoon. Well, my dear, we will be dining with the rich!' Suddenly I had visions of the afternoon just spent with Walter.

"'Mary didn't say anything about going to Swiss Chalet, did she?'"

3

CAREER CHOICES:
BE CAREFUL WHAT
YOU WISH FOR.

"Better is a handful of rest than a
double handful of hard work and
striving after the wind."— Ecclesiastes 4:6

Tim had several days to reflect on his conversation with Walter. Answers were not forthcoming. Walter certainly had indicated a casual, almost flippant outlook toward the acquiring of money. The irony was, Walter obviously had acquired a great deal of the stuff. Yet out of Walter's own mouth had come the pronouncement that in order to acquire money, most had followed the course of life of the Chans and Jacksons—working tirelessly and saving tenaciously and caring a great deal about money.

By the time Sunday morning had arrived, Tim had Walter figured out—why Walter could be so indifferent about wealth. It must be that he has always had money; not like the Jacksons and others who clawed their way into the upper class. He had always been there. Maybe Mary had come from the same social elite as well. Sure, he had spoken of Carl Jackson—being born into money—with contempt. But that was only due to the way Carl flaunted his hand-me-down riches. Walter on the other hand was discreet.

Tim had hoped to discover something about his other dinner companion, Adam Rarrie, at work. Gerry would have to know him if he had worked at Barton Brothers. Why had Adam left the store? Had he made enough to comfortably retire? Would he and Sandy be dining with four of the country's wealthy citizens? Gerry was no help. He and his wife were on an Alaskan cruise celebrating their twentieth anniversary. Tim wondered if he would be in a position to give Sandy such a gift on their twentieth. He frowned when he thought of their excursion last year for their fifth. They had made plans to go to Harrison Hot Springs for four days. He had scraped together the cost of the trip after months of saving. Twenty minutes after leaving the ferry the car had broken down. They had spent the night in the car. By the time the car had been towed to a garage and repaired they had enough money to get back on the ferry and whimper back home. Oh well, Gerry had earned this trip. He was a hard worker and had been a real teacher to Tim. Tim knew he had to pay his dues. His turn would come.

Sunday was a glorious autumn day. The on-shore breeze had died before noon, and the sun had taken advantage of the still air—drenching Victoria with all it's force and belying the claim that summer had past. As afternoon waned, their solar provider filled the western skies, then reluctantly retreated behind the San Juan Hills, leaving in it's wake the heavy air of a tropical island. Tim and Sandy strolled through the stone gates of the

Sanderson Estate soaking in their surroundings. Sandy was inclined to linger, but Tim was anxious to begin his lessons.

Walter and Mary's house looked even grander from inside. The size of the entrance with it's cathedral ceiling and semi-circular staircase was impressive, but not formal or sterile. The inlaid wood floors and wainscoting gave off a certain warmth, a feeling that they had retained a part of each of the greetings exchanged in this very room over the past hundred years. Tim imagined the setting of days gone by: friends and family—yes, even strangers—ushered in out of the night into this very room. He could hear the sound of children playing on the stairs, peering through the spindles, observing the newcomers and searching for a child with whom to play; ears fully tuned, listening to the adults, recording conversations to be replayed with their peers on later occasions. How different from today when strangers at our doors are viewed with suspicion and kept at a distance. There is a reluctance to invite such a one inside least they should look in on our private world or steal a greeting reserved for only a few.

"Come in, come in!" Mary could easily fit into Tim's scene from the past. The gentler more civilized past.

To the left was the kitchen. At one time it must have included the servants' quarters. It could easily accommodate a commercial kitchen, but for tonight it was a gathering place. "It's bigger than our apartment." Sandy whispered.

"Tim, Sandy;" Walter began, "the rest of us have started a glass of wine before supper. Except Mary, she's finished. Red or white?"

"Red please. Smells great in here." Tim was reassured by the aroma that they would not be dining out at an all- you- can- eat restaurant. So much for Walter's similarity to Mr. Jackson.

"I hope you both like shellfish. No allergies?"

"Just to the price." Tim heard himself say, then instinctively glanced at Sandy who was waiting with one of her looks.

They ate like kings: steamed mussels with creamed wine sauce, pan-fried oysters, crab newburg and mounds of steaming wild rice, baby carrots, snow peas, and fresh sour-dough bread. Tim had the presence of mind to say no to the apple crisp as it made the rounds for the second time. One serving was enough after such a feast. He didn't want to be nodding-off when Adam related his life at Barton Brothers.

They abandoned the kitchen and took coffee in the den. It was more intimate than the livingroom and had ample overstuffed chairs and couches in front of the fireplace. Tim waited for Adam and then took a chair across from his. He wanted to not only hear Adam but to watch for what wasn't said. He allowed for a few minutes of idle chatter and then began in earnest. "So Adam, Walter tells me you once worked at Barton's."

"Yes ... many years ago."

"I work there now—I think in the same department that you did. Menswear."

"Yes. Walter told me. He says you're doing well."

"Number one last month, but,.. maybe I could get some pointers from you. How long were you there? Did you like it? Why did you leave?....."

"Tim!" Sandy was embarrassed.

"I told you he was forthright, Adam." Walter joked.

"Tim, you sound a lot like me almost twenty years ago. Remember, Nancy? I'll tell you my story, but you'll have to decide whether it holds any pointers for you. I was already working at Barton Brothers when I met Nancy. Mary introduced us. They both did volunteer work at the library, teaching reading skills to adults. After we were married, we lived in my bachelor apartment for over a year. One day, out for a walk, we stumbled upon an apartment for rent downtown, in James Bay.

"'It's perfect!' I proclaimed. 'Ideal for the two of us'.

"'Two and a half.' corrected Nancy. 'It's small but the baby won't need her own room for a while.'

"'Her! Don't be calling my son a 'her'. Only one bedroom does have it's advantages like when your folks come. I'll just direct them across the street to the James Bay Inn.'

"'And the kitchen's not big enough for your mother.'

"'I think we had better call a truce.' I said. The rooms were tiny. It wasn't much bigger than my bachelor suite but a separate bedroom was a real plus. It was bright and offered glimpses of Beacon Hill Park. It felt like a real home. 'Let's take it. We only need to buy a bed. The rest of our things will fill up the space. And I can still walk to work from here.'

"Of course the clincher was the price. In 1980, $325 per month for a one bedroom in James Bay—even a tiny one bedroom, was a real find. Nancy and I watch our spending. We saw other young couples begin marriage saddled with debt. We had agreed to pay as we go. We enjoyed rummaging through yard sales. The few pieces of furniture that we had were gathered at auctions. My job didn't afford me the luxury of overspending.

"I worked evenings at Barton Brothers Department Store. Even then, it had been a fixture of the Victoria business community for three generations. The current Mr. Barton fulfilled his role gallantly as a benevolent dictator. He insisted on hiring every employee personally. He prided himself in being able to call each of the 276 employees by name. I was the janitor. I'd been there for three years, longer than I'd known Nancy. I liked the work. As I surveyed the floor I smiled with satisfaction at how it looked. The traffic marks from the day's commerce were replaced by a fresh coat of wax with it's pungent smell. Even after it dried, the scent lingered and the floor glistened. Sometimes, like the other night when Craig from the credit department was working late, an employee would hesitate to walk for fear the floor was still wet. I told Nancy about it when I came home and she said it was because everyone at Barton's thought so highly of my work that they didn't want to be the first to mar it. Nancy was always saying things like that; always building me up. She waited up for me and wanted to talk about my work. It was just cleaning; but to Nancy you'd think I had the most important job in the store. I worked til midnight. "From five to midnight, five days a week." Mr. Barton had announced when he hired me. It was only 35 hours a week at $6 an hour but I was happy. There were plenty of important things to take up the rest of the week. I liked working evenings. It left the days for living. There were quiet breakfasts together. Some days we walked. We'd walk along the waterfront in the inner harbour. Summer found the waterfront alive with people and entertainers. Buskers playing music, dancing, singing; comedians and jugglers, each trying to get the big break. A producer or agent would discover this raw talent, and they'd be on their way. Maybe he was on board one of the yachts tied up just a few yards away. Today could be the day!

"Today we took Sarah for a walk. Nancy had been right—again. Our baby was a girl; a bright, beautiful, baby girl that soon became the highlight of our lives. She was only six months old but it was hard to remember many happy times prior to her arrival. There was only a blur between the wedding and the birth of dear Sarah. The photo albums confirmed this phenomenon. Sarah enjoys our walks. Strapped securely in my backpack, she rides aloft, enjoying the rhythm of my walk. It only takes a hundred yards before she is fast asleep. Sleep reserved for children uninterrupted by the external noises and distractions of life. Sleep unaware of any future anxiety that rushes in on us in later years. Such is the sheer joy of the very young. A joy she transmits to Nancy and I as we stare in amazement at this most precious gift.

"We walk along Dallas Road with the ocean to our right. We watch the kites float in the on-shore breeze. We watch the sailboats beat against the whitecaps, their unfurled genoas straining against the wind, which is always more forceful away from the shelter of the shore. The sails always look too ungainly for the size of the ship, like children dressed up in their parents' clothes. We worry as gusts of wind threaten to knock down the sailboats, and marvel as they unfailingly right themselves. We never tire of watching the sea and all the participants, with the Olympic mountains as a backdrop. We walk along Beach Drive, past stately houses with cobblestone drives and manicured lawns. In the spring we are treated to a vista of tulips, daffodils and flowering shrubs. Little paths, wind down to the beach. Sometimes, if the tide has retreated far enough, you can walk along the shore and see these same houses from the waterside. You can see the patios and decks; the bay windows of every dimension. 'Can you imagine,' Nancy says, 'waking up to such a sight every day. I could look out those windows all day long.' But there is never anyone looking out the windows. No one sitting on the decks or patios. No one playing on the beautiful lawns. Once we had seen someone trimming the edges. He was close to where we were, and we ventured over to strike up a conversation.

"'Oh, I don't live here,' was the reply. 'I come by twice a week to do the yard work. I take my lunch on the patio—I probably use it more than the owner does. I haven't seen him all month, and his wife is out of town on business most of the time.'

"Today we sit on the rocks, at the water's edge. The tide is flooding, erasing any trace of our disturbing the beach. Shore birds come alive with nervous energy, running in tune with the tide, looking to see what the sea will serve them. Each time we watch this tidal ritual, it is as if we have discovered it for the first time. We remain motionless lest we somehow disturb the perpetual motion of the sea and all that she nurtures. These are moments to savour, to share and remember. We look up at the beautiful empty homes— no, just houses— and feel sorry for their owners who deprive themselves of such moments.

~ ~ ~

"I couldn't wait to get home. I remember taking the stairs to our apartment two at a time. 'No more cleaning floors for me!'

"'I thought you liked cleaning floors.'

"'That was yesterday. Today I'm movin on up!' I danced around our tiny home.

"'Okay, Adam, calm down before you wake the baby, and fill me in on what's behind this manic behavior.'

"'You know Charlie Saunders, in sales. He's been there forever. Always made good money too. Well today, right out of the blue, he gives his notice. Something about his family in Toronto wanting him to come back there and help run their business—dry cleaning or something.'

"'But what's that got to do with you? You haven't bought a new suit since we were married.'

"'Who is Mr. Barton's favourite employee? You know how he's always saying what a great worker I am. I'll talk with him tomorrow. I've already got Charlie on my side. He said he'd teach me before he leaves. He's got a desk drawer full of lay-downs.'

"'Lay-downs?'

"'That there's sales talk for easy sales.' My Jethro imitation only elicits a pained smile. 'I can't wait to start making some decent money. Did I tell you that Charlie brought home some serious coin? Me selling footwear and I'm a shoe-in with Mr. Barton. Get it, footwear—shoe-in?'

"'Yes dear. Can we go to bed now? It's late. Good thing there's no one trying to sleep downstairs.'

~ ~ ~

"'I don't know, Adam, you don't have any experience in sales. I've got six resumes already, and Charlie just gave his notice. Four of these guys are already in sales: vacuum cleaners, real estate... here's one who works at our competitor's.'

"'You know I'm a good worker, Mr. Barton, and a quick learner. With Charlie's help I'll catch on in no time. With a new baby, we really could use the extra money.'

"'What about cleaning the store; who could I get to replace you? The staff and our customers have come to expect the store to shine.'

"'I'll train the new guy myself; after hours, on my own time. You won't be sorry Mr. Barton.'

"And so it came about that Adam the janitor became Adam the fashion consultant. I worked hard and brought home trade journals and fashion magazines to study style and trends. I watched businessmen as they walked the streets of Victoria to see what the locals preferred. Soon I could tell a Pierre Cardin from a Ralph Lauren and a Gucci from a Rochport.

"But mostly I learned how to sell. Charlie was a great teacher and he understood what people wanted to hear. I learned how to make people feel good about themselves. I took an interest in each customer, no matter how modest their purchase was. I found out about where they lived and worked, the names of family. When they returned to pick up their altered clothes they left with a greeting for Mrs. Johnson or a 'bring Josh by next time'. Each customer went away feeling that they were the most important person to me. Indeed I might even confide in them that their purchase made a real difference in my paycheque and I'd always be grateful.

~ ~ ~

"'Look at this pay stub!' It's only been six months and I'm already earning 50 percent more than I was cleaning floors.' I was pleased with myself. 'I can't believe we ever survived on the pittance I was making scrubbing floors, emptying ashtrays, cleaning urinals.' I squirmed thinking about my former duties.

"'$800 a month sure wasn't much,' agreed Nancy, 'but we never went without. It's great having the extra money, but I do miss the mornings we used to have together.'

"'Don't forget—I had to work practically all night.'

"'Not quite all night, Adam, and you still work two evenings a week.' It's true, I was working more but only an extra 10 hours a week and look at the trade-offs. 50 percent more income. It was time to see some real benefits from our newfound wealth!

"'Honey, on my lunch break, I went to look at a two bedroom unit in the Alderlea. I want to take you to have a look tomorrow.'

"'Do you really think we can afford it?'

"'Sure. One of the guys at work lives there. He doesn't make anymore than I do. It's time Sarah had a room of her own. Right Sarah?' Sarah heard her name and added to the conversation as only an 18 month old can. I interpreted her response to be total agreement with my point of view.

"The new apartment was everything that it was advertised to be. The decision to move was immediate. Nancy was concerned about the extra $200 per month, but over the past six months our stringent budget controls had gradually relaxed. I assured her that sales were great and commissions would only go up. I lived up to my promise. Each month my pay was bigger. Our life was now sectioned into segments: the present lifestyle and 'before sales', or BS as I referred to it.

With each increase in pay there was a greater increase in deductions. In the days of BS it was simple: Unemployment Insurance premiums—$14.20, Canada Pension Plan—$7.80. Total deductions from my $800, was $22.00. For the month of October (in this new era) my earnings were$1400. Now my UI premiums were $26.20, and CPP was $16.20. With my new position came more opportunities to give. For the first time in our marriage I began contributing to the Revenue Canada team. At first it was small: ten or fifteen dollars per pay but like an insatiable addiction, the amounts grew. October was my best month to date and the government wanted to share in my success: $190.00 for Income Tax alone! Total deductions—$232.40 from $1400. Oh well this was just the price of our better standard of living. It made me feel like I had arrived. Now I could complain with the best of them about how much tax I was paying. 'Don't worry,' I assured Nancy, 'I'll just sell a couple more suits, a few more pairs of Gucci.'

"There was only one little draw back with our new apartment. It was too far from work to walk. The first time I missed the bus and was late for work, I started looking at cars. It had been five years since I had owned a car. Like every teen, impatient to become an adult, I went through the rite-of-passage: get my driver's licence, buy a beater, buy a stereo that costs one and half times the price of the beater, borrow money from my mom to fix the beater, wreck the beater, lose my licence. It took two years to get back my licence and another year to finish paying off my mom for my initiation into manhood. Now Nancy and I walk or take the bus. Occasionally we will rent a car for the weekend to go for a drive up-island. But this is different. I can think of a hundred reasons to own a car. Just last week, while coming home on the bus, someone spilled coffee on my new suit. Nancy could use the car to go help out at the library. We wouldn't need to plan so far ahead to go for a drive; we could just decide and do it. Of course there would be extra expense but my new job was equal to the task.

~ ~ ~

"New Years day and I slept till noon. December was quite a month. I worked every day except Sundays and Christmas: 25 days—12 hours a day. Sales were outstanding and I was at the head of the class. $2600 commission for the month. Mr. Barton had been gracious. 'I'm glad you listened to me, my boy, and got into sales. I knew you'd be a great success.' The words confirmed my acceptance as a salesman. The $200 bonus would go to Visa.

"Credit cards; Nancy and I had vowed never to own one.... as if anyone can really own a debt. Too many of our friends had succumbed to the lure of easy credit. With the new job came the pre-approved applications for cards. It wasn't like we would borrow on them. They would just come in handy—for emergencies. Like the time we were out with friends and everyone decided to go for pizza. $30 should have been more than enough; then someone ordered beer. I have to tell you, I was pretty embarrassed to have to borrow $10.

"And so the vow had been broken. The card had arrived. Not just any credit card—a Platinum Visa. Only a select few qualified and I had been chosen. The letter said so. With the card came the cheques. Personalized cheques ready for my signature. It was like a separate bank account with $2000 already there awaiting our instructions for use.

"It hadn't come too soon. Our new apartment looked a little bare with our few pieces of furniture from our BS days. There was little time for yard sales and auctions. Someone in my position really should be buying new furniture. Still, I was a little taken aback by the cost. Have we really spent $1500 in an afternoon? But it was a fantastic sale and the Visa will be paid off in no time.

"The bonus cheque was a full $200. No deductions. They showed up today with my regular pay. My earnings for December were $2900 with the bonus. UI premiums $48.60, CPP $42.90, Income tax $740.00! I'm stunned. There must be some mistake. I'll call personnel in the morning. Surely people can't possible pay this much to the government. What am I paying for? I understand (sort of) about Unemployment Insurance and Canada Pension. These are for me and my family, if I'm out of work or can't work or when I retire. But the tax—so much tax. If it cost me $200 to pay my share of government services last month, why does it cost me $740 for the same services this month? There must be some mistake. Wendy from personnel will straighten this out but today I need to pay some bills.

"Even after these deductions, I've still got over $2000 to work with. Okay rent is $525 and I'm sending visa $400. I've got to pay that off. The interest last month was $40. My car payment is $180 (thirty-four more to go). Car insurance is $95—I can't believe those terrorists are still holding me ransom for a few infractions almost five years ago. Where was I? Oh yes, my Barton Brother's account, it's up to $500 now with the clothes for Sarah and my new suit. I have to dress for success you know! I'd better give them $100. Nancy will need $300 this month for groceries and I'll need $150 for gas and parking. The hydro is $40 and the phone bill is $70. Seventy dollars! It would be cheaper to have Nancy's parents move in! Then there's lunches and miscellaneous—another $100. How much is all that? $1960! That's cutting it too close. Maybe I'll give Visa only $300. I'll have extra when Wendy clears up this tax thing. It's a good thing I'm not trying to juggle this on a janitor's salary.

"'Ready for our walk? You promised.' Nancy interrupted my thoughts.

"'It's been a while since we've gone for a walk. Sarah was just starting to walk and now look at her go.'

"'I've been a little busy if you haven't noticed.' I was disappointed with what had blurted out. I was thinking the same thing; how little time we had spent together the last nine months. But somehow my thoughts coming from Nancy's mouth leave me pretty defensive.

"'I wasn't criticizing, I just made an observation. I know you're working hard to take care of us and I appreciate it. I'm worried that you're working too hard.'

"'I'm sorry. Look January will be a slower month. My shifts will be back to normal and we'll have lots of time together. Just like old times.'

"My prophecy was half correct. January was slower—much slower. Sales stumbled and then ground to a halt. Mr. Barton called a staff meeting on the twelfth to announce that sales were off by 34 per cent from the same period last January. The figures and charts only put on paper what every salesperson knew. In an effort to increase sales I worked my client list feverishly. I talked to those I had inherited from Charlie but had never called before. There had been no need to call before. January drifted into February with each day seeing less traffic through the store. My commission cheque for January was a disaster. It amounted to minimum wage and was only that much because employers were required to pay the minimum. In reality, I had worked much more but that was my choice. I had pressed my nose against the window of success and was determined to gain access. I had gone to Wendy with the error on my December deduction statement and found to my utter amazement that there was no error. I sure could use the money that I gave to them in December. At least I wouldn't have that expense. With the money I'm earning this month, I won't pay a dime in income tax.

~ ~ ~

"I came home and sat in front of the television. It should have been paid for months ago. The news is on. More dire predictions for the economy. Inflation has been running out of control and the prescription to cure the problem is brutal. Like some ancient form of witchcraft that demands severe pain to the victim and human sacrifices to appease the gods of commerce. The priests read the entrails and try to predict the future. Interest rates are pushed higher, partly to slow down domestic borrowing, mostly to entice the pools of money flowing like so much sacrificial blood to be offered to the highest bidder. The governments have convinced themselves that this is their saviour and have it they must at any cost. No thought is given to the future costs. British Columbia and Alberta are leading the rest of the country into a recession. People are losing their jobs, homes, marriages. Many turn to bankruptcy while others take more desperate measures. Suicide numbers climb. 'Another bad day?' queried Nancy, 'You're awfully quiet.'

"'Remember Raymond? Mr. Barton laid him off today. He said there wasn't enough traffic to be able to afford all the salespeople in our department. I can't believe it! Ray's been there for ten years. Mr. Barton said he carried him as long as he could but the sales just aren't there. I don't know who was more upset—Ray or Mr. Barton?'

"The first half of 1983 was a right-off. Business adopted a survival code. 'Lean and Mean' was the battle cry. For some it wasn't enough. One of our competitors, Romans, withered and died. The receivers, who were enjoying a banner year in the only growth industry, began to do their work with a certain pleasure reserved for morticians and actuaries. The liquidation was aggressive. Barton Brothers may as well have closed the doors for that three weeks period. Now it was September. The back to school sales had created little interest and even fewer sales. The banks have told Mr. Barton to cut costs. The lay-offs have begun. I am outselling most in our department but barely making the cut-off for minimum wage. With the departure of Raymond, everyone fears for his job. Where is the security that we enjoyed just last year? Will Barton Brothers survive?

"It isn't just business that is running on survival instinct. We all are. Nancy offered to go back to her old job at the bank. Nancy had worked there for five years before we were married. It was strange that the banks were hiring when most businesses were scaling down. When Nancy came back from her interview, I understood. The full time jobs were being eliminated. ATM machines were replacing many tellers. They have no benefits. They never ask for holiday pay, pensions, raises or unions. The machines are perfect employees for the bank. Their human counterparts remaining would be part-time employees with slightly better working conditions and benefits than the ATMs. Nancy is a real trooper and is happy to be able to contribute to our needs. I feel miserable. We had agreed years ago that Nancy would stay home and look after Sarah. My income had been enough. Somehow we had changed our earning requirements, so that when my income fell we were quickly on the ropes. The bigger apartment, the car, the new clothes and furniture—they were all strangling us. 'It'll just be for a few months until we get over this rough spot.' Nancy consoled me. 'And it's only part-time, three days a week.'

"The extra salary was sorely needed but I was in for a surprise. Nancy works 24 hours a week and earns $8 an hour for $192. Day care for Sarah is $45. Extra car expense and buses cost $20. Nancy needs more clothes for work which averages another $20. We are both tired when we get home and end up eating out more often which costs another $30. And then there are the deductions. Nancy loses $32. a week off her cheque for UI, CPP and tax and I lose an extra $10 a week from my meagre income because I no longer claim her as a dependent. When I add the extra expense and take this off her income, I calculate that her true take home pay is $35 per week. Nancy spends 24 hours working and another 8 hours getting to and from work every week. She is bringing home just over $1 per hour! I'm sick at heart over this sacrifice but right now we need the $35. All across Victoria, possibly all over the modern world, couples are making these sacrifices to stay afloat. I don't like what is happening to my family and my co-workers.

"Monday, a man walked up to Gerry Davis and asked 'Is Adam Rarrie working today? He called and said the shoes I like are on sale this week. I told him I'd stop by.'

"Gerry hesitated. He had seen the gentleman as he entered the store. His eyes had followed him as he made his way directly to Menswear. There was a definite purpose to his stride. This fellow was here to buy. Gerry had not had many good prospects this shift—just browsers, asking questions and killing time. 'Do you have this blazer in red? Oh....you do? Well, I'll bring my wife by to have a look.' But this fellow was for real. And he was asking for Adam. Adam, who had closed three sales this shift and left for lunch not five minutes ago.

"'No I'm sorry, Mr. Rarrie is off today. We work together. May I be of service?' This wasn't Gerry, Adams co-worker and friend, speaking. It was Gerry the father and husband, with a mortgage and car payment past due. He'd always prided himself on his integrity. His words had taken him by surprise. He wanted to recant. It was too late. He had to play it through. Mr.

Walker, Adam's customer, did indeed buy the Rochport shoes. Gerry was determined to inform Adam immediately upon his return and have him receive the credit. Then Mr. Walker spotted the leather overcoat that he fancied. And the matching scarf. The pigskin gloves. The umbrella. It was too much to give up. After all, who had trained Adam after Charlie left? Who had introduced him to some wealthy customers at the last civic function? Adam would understand. 'Yeah Adam will understand,' he muttered to himself, 'I just robbed him of two hundred bucks.'

"I returned from lunch and made the usual inquiries. 'Anything going on?'

"Gerry shook his head. 'Just lookers.'

"The afternoon dragged on. Gerry was quiet. He looked defeated. 'Nothing a good day of sales won't cure.' I thought. I had been expecting Mr. Walker. I was disappointed that he didn't show but it wouldn't be the first time a customer changed his mind. Lately, that was the norm. At the end of our shift I alerted the others on the floor to let me know if they saw my Mr. Walker. Gerry didn't respond.

"Tuesday Gerry stayed home. Mr. Barton was by, making his rounds, trying to rally the troops. First the carrot then the stick—whatever would work.

"'Where's Gerry?'

"'He phoned in sick.' I offered.

"'Too bad. He had a great sale yesterday; I was hoping he could make it two in a row. Maybe the rest of you will follow his example and help pull us out of this hole.'

"I was puzzled. What was Mr. Barton talking about, Gerry having a great day. Why hadn't I noticed it? Gerry had said nothing. But it wasn't like Isaac Barton to get sales figures wrong.

"Gerry showed up Wednesday morning looking like it was hour three of a twenty-four hour flu. His eyes were red and swollen. His face was ashen and drawn. 'Gerry should you be working today?'

"'I feel awful, but I need to talk to you.'

"'Sounds serious. What's wrong?'

"'I've done something I'm not proud of.'

"'Are you sure you want to talk to me?' I didn't want to get mixed up in any domestic problems.

"'It concerns you, Adam. I've been stewing over how to tell you. There's no easy way. Your customer, Mr. Walker was in on Monday....and I sold him a few things.'

"'Oh ..... so that was the big sale that Mr. Barton was telling us about yesterday.'

"'I'm sorry. I've never done anything like that before. You know me, Adam. I was afraid. Afraid of losing my job. I'll give you the commission as soon as I can. The bank's leaning pretty heavy on me.'

"'And you want the sales credit to stay on your account. It'll look good for his lordship.'

"'Please, Adam. I need this job!'

"I turned away. For the first time in four years I had second thoughts about selling for Barton Brothers. I can roll with the ups and downs in selling. I know every month can't be Christmas season. I can even put in extra hours with no results, and still keep a positive outlook. I don't let the rejection get to me. But, I just don't think I can endure seeing what it does to men like Gerry. Decent, honest, trustworthy men.

~ ~ ~

"The economy has gradually improved. A year after that discussion with Gerry, British Columbia is on the road to recovery. Still fragile, but recovering nonetheless. Inflation is slowing down; interest rates are falling. Newcomers are again looking at B.C.—retirees from the rest of Canada and immigrants from around the world. Real estate has risen 20 percent, and once again companies are hiring. People have money to spend, and Barton Brothers is open for business. Sales are strong, my commissions are good. But the fun is gone. It's time for a change.

"I can't afford to quit. I am committed. The past three slow years have left Nancy and I on the ropes. I feel like those little boats running against the tide and wind. We had barely stayed off the rocks. We have used Nancy's connection at the bank to borrow some money to help us through. Our credit card is clear; the car loan is paid off, replaced by a $8000 loan at the bank. The used car that we bought is now three years more used. I'm hearing noises that sound expensive. Sarah's starting school and there's new clothes to buy. More Guccis to sell.

"'Honey, I'm home.' Oh yeah she's working late today, bank

audit or something. I was supposed to pick up Sarah. I'd better call the sitter. 'Hi, it's Adam Rarrie. Sorry I'm late but I'll be right over for Sarah.' I wonder how Nancy will take this work change. She knows I haven't been happy in sales the last year. She wanted me to stick with it until we get our bills paid off. But this opportunity won't be there then. Sure it's a cut in pay, but it's guaranteed salary, and I'll be off the sales floor. I'll be working with Craig, we always get along. I must remember to tell her that there will be no more shift work; straight eight to five and no weekends. I was hoping she could stop work. Maybe after the first raise. Mr. Barton said once I finish the credit manager courses I'd be in line for a raise. I don't think I'll mention the night courses for a few days. Nancy needs a while to get used to this change.

"I practiced giving my announcement for Nancy on Sarah on the way home from the sitter's, and while I made our supper, and when I put her to bed. But I couldn't answer Sarah's only question. 'When's mommy coming home?'

"'Mommy's working late. She'll be home after you go to sleep.'

"'No. I mean when is mommy coming home to stay?'

"Compared to Sarah's question, Nancy was a push over. I wasn't surprised that making less money was not a big issue with her. She was happy that I would be working fewer hours. She didn't even mention her job. I know she wants to be home with Sarah, but we both know that the money she earns is all spoken for. Nancy now earns $240 a week. Of course the expenses are all higher but at least we get to keep $70. We don't keep it long, it goes right back to the bank on our loan. If I was making the kind of money that Craig is making, Nancy could stay home and we'd be free of the bank. Craig must be close to retirement. When he goes, I'll step into his job as Credit Manager. These past few years will all be a distant memory.

~ ~ ~

"It's been a hectic eighteen months since I left the floor. I didn't realize how much time and energy a few night courses consume. It all sounded so simple: Tuesdays and Thursdays, two hours a night. But if you want to pass the exams, there's a lot of studying. And when you're not studying, you're thinking you should be studying. It took a whole year, but I've done it. And Mr. Barton was true to his word—I got my raise. I remember that first December in sales when I made $2900. I was on the top of the world. Now I'm making $2000 every month, and it doesn't seem like so much. I can't believe Nancy's still working! We earn $3400 a month. The government says we're middle class. They reward us by taking away the child tax credit and increasing our medical premiums. We now contribute $780 every month to Revenue Canada, $85 to UI, and $75 to CPP. A union has found it's way into the bank, to protect the part-time jobs and add to my wife's expenses—another $20 per month. Add to this the $72 for medicare and we take home $2368 a month. Our apartment has experienced substantial appreciation with the turning of many such units into condominiums. The owners have opted to continue renting the units but our rent is now $750—still a fair price in the marketplace. My worries about our car last year were well founded. We now own a one year old van. The dealer was kind enough to take our car in trade and allow us $2,000 on a $15,000 vehicle. Unfortunately we had spent $1500 on our car before we decided to unload it. The van payments are $400 per month for the next four years. The insurance company finally gave me a discount for my reformed driving record. This discount was offset by a higher rating of our new vehicle. The result? Monthly auto insurance is now $90 per month. Our day care expenses are the best deal. We pay the same as when Nancy returned to work, because Sarah is only there a few hours after school. It still amounts to $150 per month. Our grocery bill is the same—$300. We have two more box stores in Victoria. We no longer have the wonderful little community stores to cater to our needs, but we only pay $12 for a turkey that cost a farmer $14 to grow. You can't stand in the way of progress. It's too bad that the farmers and the Costcos couldn't do the same for our gasoline. It now costs us $150 to drive for a month. We're still paying the bank $300 per month, but with car repairs and other regular emergencies, the loan balance hasn't diminished by much. Our hydro bill is $50. The phone bill at $40 is actually less than five years ago. We still eat out twice a month at Milo's, and Sarah insists on growing out of her clothes with some regularity. This adds another $100 to our monthly expenses and I've got to admit we flitter away extra cash on things like toothpaste and medicine (mostly headache pills). I saw Craig's pay stub yesterday. He's making double my wage. I should ask him how long he plans on hanging around at Barton's.

~ ~ ~

"Craig Smith decided not to hang around much longer. On February 12th I found him slumped over his desk. He died of an aneurism. The man was 56 years old! I thought he was 65. How could he look so old, and die so young? A few days after the funeral Nancy and I went over to see Connie, his widow. We had been at their house on a couple of occasions. Craig had hosted catered affairs and was known as a big spender. Even with his salary, I wondered how he managed. He lived in Cordova Bay—a good neighbourhood. Their house was beautifully furnished with wool carpets and Queen Anne pieces that we admired. The three car garage housed an 18 foot Trophy Bayliner and a vintage MGB. When we arrived, Craig's Beemer wasn't in the driveway, but we surmised that it was in the garage. Connie confided in us that the dealer had been by to re-possess it. He was three months behind on his lease payments. Craig had been living on borrowed time with borrowed money. Both Craig and his wife were aware of his high blood pressure. She had cautioned him to slow down and live more simply. Craig was proud of his position at Barton's and in the community. He told his wife that it was expected of someone in his position to have the sports car, the boat, the nice home, the winter excursions to Hawaii and Mexico. He never had the time to put the boat in the water. The MGB hadn't been licenced in two years. He worried while on vacation about how to step off the treadmill. Years ago he could have done it, but as the treadmill went faster and faster there was no way off without falling and embarrassing himself in front of his colleagues. I asked Connie how she would manage. Would there be enough money to hold onto the house? What about life insurance? Yes she had the policy through work and someone from the club had sold Craig a $200,000 policy years ago. It was so expensive that he let it go after a year. Craig had kept the document. Another fake prop. His friends needn't know it was not in force. Connie wasn't concerned about what the people at their club thought. She would sell all the props that supported Craig's lifestyle. She would be content with less.

"Nancy and I drove silently back to our home. For the first few blocks I thought about Craig. What a waste! True, no matter how he lived, he might have died young. But look what he missed out on while he was alive. Surely he didn't plan to live that way. How and when did it start? Am I on that same treadmill? The rest of the trip home I thought about Raymond.

"'Remember Raymond, the fellow I worked with on the floor? Remember I told you about him getting laid off?'

"'What about him?'

"'I saw him at Craig's funeral. It's been four years and he looks better than I've ever seen him look.'

"'What do you mean better?'

"'Better, happier.....younger even. Yeah, younger. He was

telling me that getting laid off was the best thing that ever happened to him. Can you believe it! Here I was, thinking Ray had been a casualty of the last recession; yet he's made out great. At the same time I've been wanting to be like Craig, and ...... There is no need to finish the comparison. Ray had taken stock of his goals and priorities when he lost his job. He realized that he had the most important pieces to a happy life. A good wife, his health and self respect. He just needed to earn a living. He looked at how much he really needed and found that it was much less than he had been chasing after. So Ray simplified things. He sold his house and second car, paid off his bills, and started again. How many of us get a chance to begin anew with that kind of wisdom? I was a sceptic. 'Love don't pay the rent, Ray.' But he reminded me just how little we really need, if we have no bills and choose to live simply. I started remembering about our earlier days of marriage. I used to joke about them as being BS days. But they were happy days. We had more time, less pressure. The days before bank loans and gas increases and Revenue Canada. I'm tired of you working, tired of not having time for you or Sarah. I miss the walks together along the ocean. I don't want our home to be like those empty houses we use to see along the beach. I'm getting off this treadmill. Now!'

Nancy had been waiting for just such an announcement. The next day we started to simplify. We cut our cable-vision and started looking for a smaller, cheaper apartment close to my work. We found one just a block from where we had been when Sarah was born. I sold the van for what we owed on it and we invested in a one month bus pass for Nancy. When the month was up, Nancy was finished work. We canceled Sarah's spot at day care and took half of the money that we would save next month and went to Milos to celebrate. Six months later we were out of debt and I went to see Mr. Barton.

"'Mr. Barton, I can't live on what you're paying me.' I began. He assured me that I was making the same salary that Craig had made.

"'Mr. Barton, you're paying me too much money. To earn this much money I have to work longer than I want to. This takes too much time from living. I'm missing out on the joys of life—therefore, I can't live on what you're paying me.'

"Talk about your Kodak moment. I stayed long enough for Barton Brothers to hire a new Credit Manager. It didn't take long. I had twenty-eight resumes on my desk in three days, all of the applicants more qualified than I. It's amazing how many people can't wait to jump on that treadmill.

"I never got to draw any insurance from my Unemployment Insurance plan. The day after I left Barton Brothers, I bought a ladder, bucket, sponge and squeegee and started cleaning windows. My first account was Barton Brothers Department Store. That afternoon when Sarah came home from school we went for a walk along Dallas Road and watched the boats."

~ ~ ~

Tim sat dumbfounded. He had arrived expecting to hear some profound truth that would advance his career, one of the building blocks for his financial plan. He had been prepared to revise his plan based on his conversation with Walter. Now he was asked to question the value of his career. First, he had some questions of his own. "Adam, what happens if and when—you know. The financial planners that sell life insurance ask 'what happens if you die—do you leave your family destitute?' The financial planner selling investments asks 'what happens when you get old—do you leave your family and yourself destitute?' And, Walter, don't tell me that you wash windows to pay for this place—or even for supper?

"Good questions, Tim," Adam replied, "But I think it's time for someone else to talk. Walter, your turn."

"Who wants coffee? I'll tell you all about the house over a fresh pot." Walter promised as he got up and went to the kitchen.

~ ~ ~

We need to call a time out, jump on Free Parking and think about our goals and priorities to reach these goals. Surely only a vulgar minority would list the acquiring of an abundance of money as a goal—at least in public. Ask a young married couple. Their quest is for happiness, good health, and perhaps the pursuit of humanitarian or spiritual endeavours. But hardly money for money's sake.

In order to achieve these goals most of us must allocate a portion of our lives to secular work in exchange for money. Hopefully, our work is enjoyable and meaningful, even fulfilling; but, nevertheless, it's just work. It's just a means to an end.

Imagine a month long vacation in Europe. You've planned and saved for years. You have arranged for a Euro-pass for travel. You've got all the brochures for the great museums and cathedrals memorized. Your passports are in order, and you've been punctured for every known ailment in the civilized world. You board the 767 for a 8 hour flight to Amsterdam. You've never flown this far before, and it's exciting. The flight is enjoyable, the passenger next to you is engaging, and the food is first class. They even show a movie that you haven't seen before. The captain honours you by announcing your name over the public address system, and asks you to join him in the cockpit. In no time instructions are given to return to your seat in preparation for landing. Applause breaks out as the aircraft makes a perfect landing and taxis to the terminal building. You are having such a good time that you decide to forfeit your vacation and stay on the plane! Quick, get the passenger next to you to slap you on the side of the head. The flight is just a small part of the vacation; there's much more to life than your job even if you do call it a profession or career.

Somehow society has fooled us into believing that our job is the important part of life. Work has become the definition of our being. We label people by their work. Ask you neighbour who he is and he identifies himself as a doctor or lawyer—sorry, wrong neighbourhood—bus driver or mechanic. What's wrong with: "Hey did you meet our new neighbour, Bill. He's a father." When we identify people by their occupation, what happens to people when they are laid off. They frantically search for a new job, not just for the money but to regain their identity. Does this not explain why business executives who are multi-millionaires, scramble to re-enter the workforce after being forced out? Their previous career may have cost them their health, their family and certainly their allegiance. Now, instead of feeling like Raymond in Adam's story who was relieved, the executive wants to suffer some more.

A further symptom of this malady is to qualify our occupation. We rate the significance of one's identity in dollars. We keep score with our peers. We compare salaries, bonuses, stock options, pension benefits, corner offices, company cars, even company parking spaces. (No thanks, I've already got my parking space and it's free.) A more subtle way is to tell whoever will listen how much taxes you pay or how much alimony you dole out. You can complain about the property taxes you pay or the price of getting your foreign car repaired. This all signals to your listeners, if they haven't left in boredom, that you obviously can afford this outrageous amount, and therefore, you must be better than they are.

Or you could say nothing and just accumulate items from the rich and famous catalogue. That will give everyone fair notice the you are someone of substance who commands respect. Tim feels that way about Walter.

4

POSSESSIONS:
SAY GOODBYE
TO THE JONESES

"Sweet is the sleep of the one serving...
but the plenty belonging to the rich is
not permitting him to sleep."— Ecclesiastes 5:12

We live in a world in which people are possessed with the acquiring of possessions. It is claimed that it takes a lot to shock New Yorkers. In 1980, many in this city were shocked to hear that a local couple had entered a car dealership with the intent of trading their infant child for a used sports car. The police were alerted; and they waited as the couple returned with the baby and signed the documents to complete the transaction.

An isolated incident? Naturally. But it does highlight the value that some put on possessions. The expression "keeping up with the Joneses", coined in a past generation, has taken on new meaning. There is a rush to not just keep up, but to get ahead of the Joneses or the Wangs or anyone else that is in our circle of influence. We measure this competition in terms of things, what we have, especially what we have that others can see. Our house is almost forty years old. It has a one car garage. Houses built in the seventies and eighties had two car garages; and, over the last number of years, the three car garage has been en vogue. A very visible sign for all to see in the game of one-upmanship.

Speaking of houses, we left our three couples in Mary and Walter's house. Walter had promised to reveal to Tim how he managed to acquire such a house, while espousing the values of a simple life. Tim was ready for anything. After all, he had just received a lesson on ambition from a window washer.

"Now Walter, I think you've kept this poor man in suspense long enough. Go ahead and tell Tim and Sandy how we happen to be in this house." Mary could sense that Walter was enjoying this evening; watching Tim's face as his mind downloaded all of the information provided by Adam's experience. There were moments when Tim's eyes had revealed that he was sure of the next sequence of events, only to be followed by his mouth gaping open in disbelief.

"I'm afraid I won't be able to compare with Adam's tale. Mary's and my story doesn't have a death scene, but watching Adam, Nancy, and little Sarah over these past twenty years did have an effect on us. We had already embraced a simpler way of life and when we saw the benefits that our friends were reaping, we knew that we weren't unique. It will work for anyone. You might have guessed, Tim, that I enjoy watching people—people like Mr. Chan and Mr. Jackson. But I also took note of the Art Thompsons and the Marty Dunlaps. These two were about as different from Mr. Jackson and Mr. Chan as you could get. I never saw Art do a lick of work, and I knew him for over twenty years. He said he hurt his back when he was young—playing ball. I think he played in a Triple A league. He collected a small disability pension from the government, and folks use to give him things and have him over for a meal. He'd tell them stories—he could tell great stories. Then Art would thank his generous hosts and go home to a little trailer at the edge of town. His hosts would shake their heads, saying you couldn't believe a word that Art said, as they locked their doors for the night. When I was in school, Art was the most popular guy in town. At least to us kids. He was always at the ball games or the hockey rink. He never missed a game. All the guys couldn't understand why our dads couldn't be there. He knew all the big league ball players, told us how he'd helped some of them when they were in a slump. I wanted my dad to be just like old Art Thompson. Then I got a little older. Art Thompson didn't look the same to me after awhile. For the first time, I listened to the whispers when folks saw Art come to town. They said he wasn't injured, but just lazy and shiftless. Shiftless—folks used to say that word quite a bit when they talked about Art. Now when I saw Art at the games, I saw him different than before. Now I was glad he wasn't my dad. But I still liked his stories. I just didn't believe them all— like before. One day, when a bunch of us were standing outside the pool hall, we saw old Art starting to cross the street. One of the fellows started to call him over so he could tell us about Mickey Mantle or Roger Clements. Suddenly, I was telling the others that I wasn't hanging around to listen to anymore lies from Art.

'He's shiftless.' I said. I didn't even know what it meant. I'd heard everyone else say it, and I knew by the way they said it that it's not something you'd call your friend. Art Thompson had been my friend. I went home and climbed into bed. My mom called me for supper, but I told her I was sick. I was sick—I threw-up. I made a promise to myself—with my head hanging lifelessly in the toilet—that I would never again say or do anything just because everyone else said it was so.

"The next morning, Saturday, I was standing outside Art's trailer knocking on his door. Art came out after a considerable time, standing in his long-johns, rubbing the sleep from his eyes. It was after eight, but I could tell this was not his usual waking-up hour. I apologized for waking him and then told him what I said yesterday and then apologized all over again. I told him I had no business calling him shiftless and I knew he was hurting too bad to hold down a regular job. And I told him I'd like to be his friend again, if he'd let me, and I didn't care what anyone said, 'cause I knew all his stories were true.

"Art just smiled, with what teeth he had left, and invited me inside. He pushed an old matted cat off a kitchen chair and sat down. He motioned for me to pull up the only other chair. Art probably wasn't in the habit of entertaining. His place was dingy and had a peculiar odour that my mom said she could still smell on my clothes after several washings. He didn't offer me anything, for which I was thankful.

"'So folks think I'm shiftless, do they? Well, I'll tell you something, Wally. I got my place here, and the guy from the gas company stops by once a month and makes sure I got propane.

I sign for it, and away he goes. Same thing for my lights. When I want food, I take in a voucher, and Harry Vos gives me my groceries. Why in creation would anyone work when you got this going for you? I may be shiftless, but the rest of this town is just plain dumb.' And with that he pried a glass off the table, that had been doing it's best to put down roots in last night's left-overs, poured himself a drink of rum, and toasted the morning.

"I went home and pulled down Mr. Webster's dictionary from the top shelf. I looked up 'shiftless'. It could have had a picture of Art Thompson for a definition. This time, I didn't listen to the crowd. I came to the same answer, but I did my own thinking. Art was wrong. You weren't stupid because you wanted to work; to provide for yourself and family. Work is good. But could too much work be just as bad as not working? Couldn't there be some sort of balance? Maybe my dad couldn't get to most of the games, because of work; but could he not get to one?

"I met Marty Dunlap when he first came to town about a year after my encounter with Art and his trailer. Folks just said he was another Art Thompson, and one Art was too many. This time I wasn't listening. The truth was, Marty was different from most people. For one thing, he rode a bicycle. Today many adults ride bikes, but back then only kids rode bikes, at least in our town. And he didn't have a 'real' job. One day he'd till Mrs Johnson's garden. The next week he'd be mowing a lawn or cleaning out eaves troughs. I often saw him alongside the highway, picking up empty bottles. No. He wasn't a bit like Art

Thompson. He worked—not like Dad or the other fathers—at real jobs—but he worked. And he also came out to watch us play ball. He'd be sitting there beside Art and all the moms, cheering the home team. Marty didn't know much about baseball, but he always had a good time. Come to think of it, Marty had a good time all the time. It didn't matter whether he was cleaning up someone's yard, painting a shed or picking up bottles, Marty was smiling. And when he wasn't smiling, he was whistling or singing. I never met a happier guy. People couldn't understand. How could he be so happy when he had nothing? No regular job, no car, just a few tools and that silly bicycle. Folks all called him simple and said, 'He's more to be pitied than laughed at.' In our town they were always summing up others by some saying that they labeled you with. It clung to you like dandruff on the shoulders of your best suit. You could try your best to brush it off, but it would be back.

"I would take Marty a paper when I had an extra after my route. He was happy to get the weekend paper and it didn't even matter if it was a day late. Marty was interested in what was going on in the world, but he didn't have to be the first one to know. I liked going over to Marty's. He rented a tiny apartment above the drug store. It wasn't any bigger than Art Thompson's trailer, but it sure was different. Everything was neat and clean—not that there was a lot of 'everything'. Marty used to say that if he ever got more junk than he could carry on his bike, it was time to have a yard sale. He told me folks bought stuff and then never had the time to use it and I knew it was true. But not Marty, he used his things almost every day.

His big armchair, his radio, his tools, his bicycle. The thing he liked to use the most was his fishing pole. He always had time for fishing. If it was fishing season and you hadn't seen Marty doing chores for the neighbours or watching a ball-game then you could bet he'd be fishing. When my paper route was done, I'd wander over to the river and look for Marty. I don't ever remember much about the fish, but we sure had great talks. I remember asking him why he didn't have a regular job, like most folks.

"'When I was a kid, my mother used to read from the Bible, about a time coming when people would be throwing their gold and silver into the streets. My mom figured this time was coming any day now. So I thought there would be no use getting a wack of money, just to throw it away. I decided to earn just enough to get by, and spend the rest of my time living. By the time I figured out that we might have to wait awhile before we start tossing the gold and silver, it was too late. I was enjoying myself too much to ruin it all by working nine to five.'

"I went home and told my mom that I was going to be just like Marty when I finished school next year. She got all red in the face and started telling me that that was the craziest thing I'd ever said and, if I ever mentioned it again, she'd tell my father. She muttered about what the townspeople would say about me being 'more to be pitied than laughed at'. I reminded her that tag was for Marty and they'd have to come up with a new one for me.

'Well, I did mention it again, and she did tell my father. I felt bad for Dad. When he was growing up, he wanted to go to university and come out a dentist. There was no money, so he went to work in the bush, like most of the town. He made a good living for our family but he never forgot wanting to be a dentist. He'd come home after work, wet and tired, smelling of cedar and chain-saws, and talk of how much easier a life it would have been to be a dentist. He had long since decided that I would be the dentist that he couldn't be. It didn't matter that I fainted when I saw a needle—I would get used to it. That's what all those years in university would accomplish.

"Now his only son, the designated dentist, was talking about dropping out of university before he even started. For what? To mow lawns and paint outhouses! He did the only thing he could do. He called the principal. Mr. Thackerty was a principal's principal. He had been in the military, and had forgotten that he had been discharged. He had rules for every conceivable act and would recite them to the entire class, at the slightest provocation. If you got him going at the beginning of the period, you could waste the full forty-five minutes. This accounts for why I can never remember what subjects he taught.

"'Your Dad tells me you're giving up an opportunity to go to university so that you can become a bum like Art Thompson.'

"'No. I want to live like Marty Dunlap, a simpler life.'

"'Same thing. Can't you see that Mr. Dunlap has wasted any potential he had? What kind of life is tilling gardens and cleaning eaves? Don't you want to get ahead and make something out of yourself?'

"In the end, I couldn't convince Mr. Thackerty that I could

become someone without a university education, without assigning my future to a nine to five job or profession. And why all this concern about 'getting ahead'? Ahead of what—or is it ahead of whom? Must we affirm our self importance at the expense of others? Is life a competition with our peers in which only the victors are considered 'a success'? Mr. Thackerty told my Dad that my only hope was to join the army, where they could knock some sense into me.

"For the rest of the year I apprenticed under Marty Dunlap. I helped him with his odd jobs and even joined him on his 'bottle route'. He taught me how to trim a hedge and prune trees, to let the right amount of light in. He taught me how to tie a fly and how to whistle. He taught me how to live. Some afternoons we would watch crows open nutshells. To this day I am fascinated at their ability to use us to work for them. They place walnuts and acorns on city streets and wait for cars to crush them. Then, like any suburbanite picking up a pizza, they stroll over and pick up lunch. We sat down by the river and watched coons fishing for fresh water clams and crayfish. We studied spiders constructing engineering masterpieces without blueprints, and ants transporting heavy loads over long distances to benefit not just themselves but the community. If one was injured or exhausted, co-workers would come to his aid, helping him back to the colony. It takes time to acquire an education like Marty's; time was the possession he treasured the most. Over the years he had acquired a fair amount of it.

"After graduation, I said my good-byes and moved to

Victoria. Using the skills I had developed working with Marty, I soon had a little business going. I purposely kept it small. If the job was too demanding, I was happy to turn it over to one of the many property maintenance companies. They often returned the favour, putting me in touch with customers who needed only small jobs done. That's how I met Mr. Higgins.

"Mr. and Mrs. Higgins owned this very house for over forty years. He had inherited it from his uncle. It was known as 3600 Beach Drive. Mr. Higgins and his wife were in their seventies when I first met them. They needed someone to look after the lawn. It wasn't a very big lawn, then. There used to be two other properties next door that have since been added to make this present estate. In the summer, starting about the middle of May, I would mow it every week. Then, after the end of September, I would come by every two or three weeks and tidy-up—rake up any fallen branches and leaves—that sort of thing. We became good friends. I didn't have any family close by and the Higgins' only child—a daughter—was married to some executive for an environmental organization and spent most of her time in Europe. Mr. Higgins' family had made their money in coal in the British Isles; he was proud of it. I don't imagine his daughter had the same affection for this legacy.

"Shortly after I started working for Mr. Higgins I met Mary. Within a year we were married. My family came down for the wedding. My Dad and Mom, all my uncles and aunts and dozens of cousins—they were all there. You should have seen their faces when they saw my best man—Marty Dunlap. By this time Marty was over sixty, still smiling, still whistling, still learning about life. Just before he left for home, I took him around to some of the jobs. I was proud to hear him comment on my work. It was really a reflection on Marty's own skills and teaching. I asked him if he thought I could keep my same attitude toward work, now that I had Mary to support. He told me that he'd never had that responsibility but there was no sense worrying about it. I'd know soon enough. He said that we all spend too much time worrying about things that never happen and it seemed like a lot of bother and waste of time. Like so many other things that Marty had said over the years, I knew it to be true.

"Mary and I talked about our finances and decided that we would wait before we took on more work. I was working three days a week. Before we were married, Mary had been working part-time and volunteering at the library. We decided that my work could support us for now and Mary would quit her job. She still went to the library and she'd work along with me from time to time. The rest of the time we had to ourselves. Following in the footsteps (or rather bicycle tracks) of Marty, we bought bikes that we found at yard sales. In less than two years, we had found every side street and back-alley from James Bay to Broadmead. Summer days linger on when you're pedaling along—not like when your driving, all in a hurry, rushing to get to the next set of lights so you can wait. And people are different. They stop you to give a greeting or ask directions. Any excuse to engage in conversation with a kindred spirit, set apart from the polluting menaces so close at hand.

"Our bicycling excursions became less frequent when the children arrived. The first two, eighteen months apart, signaled a move to a bigger apartment. I found it necessary to add another day's work to my schedule to accommodate the increase in expenses. The children added another dimension to our lives— a fuller, richer life that more than compensated for the extra day's work. Besides, it gave me an excuse to be seen lying on the grass, in the middle of a work day, watching ants and beetles. If there is a young child watching with you, you need answer less questions about your sanity.

"It was about this time that Mr. Higgins called me to drop by 3600 Beach Drive for a talk. I had been concerned about my old friend. His wife had died suddenly six months earlier. They had been married for fifty-three years. How do you stop caring for and talking to someone after fifty-three years? You don't, and I often heard Mr. Higgins talking to his wife, as though she was still there walking beside him, holding his hand, as I had seen them a hundred times before. Sometimes he would notice me, and the reality would seize him. You could see it mostly in his eyes as they misted over with quiet resignation and loss.

"'I've decided to sell the old place.' Mr. Higgins spoke with resolve. 'It's too big to care for. It's bleeding me dry. I had to get the plumber in this week, and last month it was the roofing company.'

"'Where will you go? This house has been your home for a long time.'"

"'It was *our* home. It's not the same with Pearl gone. And my daughter's not interested in the place. Too busy saving the world. I'll find a small place right in town, close to the doctor and hospital and ....' Mr. Higgins didn't carry the chain of events any further. It wasn't the money. He would easily have spent the money on his beloved Beach Drive if Pearl had been there by his side. He had doted on the old home. It was an extension of his caring for his wife. But all of that had changed. His life had lost any purpose, any forward momentum. The future had died with Pearl. Days were filled with dwelling in the past. Had they really spent fifty-three years together? It wasn't enough, not nearly enough. Suddenly, I had the urge to run home to Mary and the kids. Life was too fragile to be handled without care. The future was too limited to be squandered on anything but living.

"'Will you sell through a realtor?'

"'One has already called me. Said he had someone interested. He wants to bring him by tomorrow. I wanted to let you know, just in case...' he paused as if only now realizing what he was contemplating. 'Just in case some fool offers me more money then this albatross is worth. It involves you, Walter. You've been caring for the grounds for years. You've done a great job, but more than that, you're a friend. Pearl was very fond of you and Mary. I hate to think of you losing the work. What am I rambling on about? Who's going to buy this place? Who else would be stupid enough to keep throwing good money after bad?'

"Mr. Higgins called later in the week to say that the realtor had brought over just such a fool. The buyer was really a corporation with it's head office in California. Mr. Higgins only met the company's agent. They had already quietly bought up the two other adjacent properties and quickly set about to merge the three. Two months after our conversation about his selling the house, Mary and I helped Mr. Higgins move into his new condo on Richmond Avenue, two blocks from the Royal Jubilee Hospital. It was his last residence.

"Mr. Higgins had offered my name as someone to continue caring for the grounds of 3600 Beach Drive. The agent, a Mr. Jenkins, arranged to meet me on the grounds the day the company took possession. He led me inside the house. It was odd, being in these familiar surroundings without the company of the Higgins. Most of their furniture was still there. They held memories that Mr. Higgins could no longer reflect on. He couldn't look at the Victorian settee without asking why Pearl wasn't sitting there. When he was in the kitchen he could still see the home made bread on the table. It was so real he could smell it. Like he could smell her powder as he passed the night stand in their bedroom. No, there were too many memories. The furniture would stay in the house.

"Mr. Jenkins spread a set of landscape blueprints on the table. The house would remain intact. The cottages on the other properties were to be razed and the grounds extended to the present size. It was to become a much larger job then I had been accustomed to doing.

"'When can you start?' Mr. Jenkins was all business.

"'It's much more work than I can take on. I never spend more than one day a week on the present grounds.'

"'And the other six days?'

"'Three belong to my family. The other three days I look after the rest of my customers.'

"'We want you here for the full seven days. Your customers can find someone else. I've done some checking around and you're the man for the job.'

"'I'm afraid you haven't checked at the right places, Mr. Jenkins, if you think I'm going to work for you or anyone else seven days a week.' I was annoyed that anyone would suggest such a thing. My determination to keep my life uncluttered was further strengthened by watching Mr. Higgins these past six months. I was seeking ways of working less, not more.

"'Now, Mr. Sanderson, hear me out. The corporation that I represent bought this property as a business decision. They foresee doing business in Canada, particularly Western Canada, and so it only makes sense to have a presence here. We know it's only a residence, but it's an address to include on correspondence with Canadian governments and companies. It's important how that address looks— call it street appeal. We would like you to help us be a good neighbour by expanding the grounds, like in the blueprints. We don't expect you to work seven days a week, but we would like you to be on the property every day. In effect, we want you and your family—your wife's name is Mary and you have two little girls—right? to move in here to 3600 Beach Drive.'

"'Move in! And what happens when the people from Head Office arrive?'

"'Relax. The third floor is twice as big as your apartment. This will be your personal area, off-limits to any staff. We'll make any renovations to make you comfortable. The rest of the house is yours to use while our people are away. Initially, you'll see someone here once a month for a couple of days. In a few months, when the novelty wears off, these guys will forget all about 3600 Beach Drive. After that some exec with his wife will fly in once every six months, you'll pick them up at the airport, drive them back three or four days later and forget about them. Oh, I've arranged for a car to be at you disposal. You do have a licence?'

"'Didn't you find that out?' I couldn't help highlighting one area that Mr. Jenkins had forgotten. He was all business. I wondered if his family knew where he was?

"Mr. Jenkins knew these people. Just as he calculated, there was a flurry over the first few months as each executive came to check out their new acquisition. They flew in; I picked them up as they complained about the small airport with no VIP lounge. We drove to Beach Drive which took half an hour, long enough to ask : "Does it ever stop raining?" Upon seeing the grand old house, restored in all her glory, the most usual comment was: "Is this all? I would have thought it would be larger." Few of these executives ever stayed long enough to follow the steps down to the shore. Fewer still sat on the beach and watched the constant motion of the sea, all the while, being caressed by the breeze that smelled of salt and kelp. They would wrap up their tour with a visit downtown which always included a stop at the Empress Hotel. There would be a less than flattering comparison with an establishment in Bel Aire. The best part was the trip back to the airport. Our guests were happy to be going back to California and we were more than happy to oblige.

"The exception to this behaviour is Mr.Clay. He's a senior vice president and he loves Victoria. He's about the only one that comes around anymore. I'm sure they would have sold Beach Drive if it wasn't for Mr. Clay. He's the reason Mary and I have our little cottage. A dozen years ago Mr. Clay's daughter was getting married. She married a guy from Vancouver and it was decided to have a garden wedding at Beach Drive. There was only one awkward area in the arrangements. The Clay's had been through a messy divorce and both were vying to stay at Beach Drive but neither would stay if the other was there. In a compromise, that only a lawyer could negotiate, it was agreed to build the cottage on the premises and the ex-Mrs. Clay and her new husband would stay there for the week of the wedding. After the wedding, Mr. Clay was about to have the cottage destroyed when I prevailed upon him to let Mary and I use it. After the kids left we decided to move in. It was easier to keep than our quarters on the third floor. We still use the house on occasion but the cottage is more our style."

~ ~ ~

"You don't own this house." Tim's words were slowly tumbling out one at a time, as if they had made a long journey from the recesses of the mind and only now as they reached the light had they come to life. "You don't own the house." he repeated. "And the Lincoln, and the cottage, and the boat tied at the dock."

"The canoe's ours!" Mary announced proudly. "But you were thinking of the Boston Whaler, weren't you?"

"What about supper? Does the company buy everything?" Tim wanted to see how far this arrangement went.

"No. Supper was on us. But it didn't cost much. Adam and I went out this morning and caught the crabs. We picked the oysters and other shellfish last week when we were 'up-island'. The rest came from Mary's garden. It really doesn't cost much to eat well, if you choose what's available locally. And there's no shortage of gourmet food right in our 'back yard'."

"Walter and I decided years ago," Mary began, "that we wouldn't want the expense and worry of everything around us even if they gave it to us." With the house comes the maintenance. The bigger the house, the greater the maintenance. Every time the wind blows you wonder if a branch will damage the roof or break a window. When it happens, Walter fixes it but the company pays. When we send the tax bill to the company every year, we count our blessings that this place isn't ours. When the muffler goes on the car, or the insurance is due, we are reminded why we don't own one. Do you know, I read somewhere, that the average driver in Victoria drives under two miles each trip? Do you really need a car for that? Most people say that they don't have the time to walk or take the bus or bike to work or to the store. If they didn't have to work all those extra hours to pay for their car, wouldn't they have plenty of time? Consider what it costs to own a car. The interest paid on money borrowed, the insurance, depreciation, the taxes, the gas, the parking, the repairs, they all add up. The average family spends over $500 per month on vehicles. If you make $20 per hour and it costs you $6 per hour to earn that money, by way of taxes and other expenses, you need to work 36 hours every month just to own a car. When you think that for every hour you work you spent another ten minutes getting ready for work and commuting to work, you come to realize that you are spending over 40 hours every month to own the car; not to mention the time you spend on washing and general maintenance. That's a lot of time that you could use to walk to the corner store for a quart of milk. Better still, Wally and I walk to the store together."

"And it's not just cars that Canadians are in love with." Adam was ready to join the conversation. "Statistics Canada says that 99% of us own colour television and half of us own at least two of them. Indeed we own more televisions than telephones. And 74% are hooked up to (or should I say hooked on) cable that we spend another $35 a month on. That's another 3 hours working to pay for this. Add that to the 70 hours a month watching television and you know where the time has gone. If we have anymore time or money left we rent videos. Over 85% of homes have a vcr.

"When you add the other gadgets, such as microwave ovens, computers, espresso machines and dishwashers, you have a picture of North Americans being suffocated in their own homes by costly, time consuming devices. Devices that we have added to the ever growing list of needs. A century ago the needs list consisted of less than half a dozen items, now it is closing in on fifty. Items that cost time, time to purchase, to use, to repair and to haul to the dump to add to the land fill. The surprising thing is that most of these items are owned not by just the affluent but also by the poorest of Canadian households. Maybe it's time we reassess our list of needs."

Sandy had been a passive observer. It was her turn to direct a question. "I'm interested, Mary, in what you mentioned about not owning a house. I understand about the extra expenses and worry, but what happens when you are ready to put your feet up? Every financial plan that Tim and I have looked at puts a high priority on home ownership. You can sell it at retirement and turn that asset into ready cash. Without this asset, how will you and Walter ever be able to retire?"

"Yeah, Walter, what's your plan? Have you been stashing money in mutual funds or treasury bills? Come to think of it, you haven't made much money to stash away have you Walter?"

"Remember, Tim, when you and Sandy first met Mary and I, ten years ago. I think you figured that we were already retired. I hope it wasn't that we looked that old."

"Oh no! Until now we always felt that you had so much money that you no longer needed to work. It's just that you were never in a hurry and we never saw you working. I mean you were always doing something but it didn't seem like work, more like a hobby. I can see now that you were working. A fellow couldn't ask for a better job."

"Well, Tim and Sandy," continued Walter, " we'll get to our retirement after a bit. But let's talk about investments for a few moments."

5

FINANCIAL FABLES:
PART 1 -- INVESTMENTS

"For where your treasure is,
there your heart will be
also." — Matthew 6:21

Financial planners are a very complex lot. Who else could sit down and tell you that the country is so mismanaged that you must take immediate steps to prepare for your retirement because the Old Age Security program and Canada Pension Plan will be broke; and in less time than it takes to read this long-winded sentence, they tell you that the economy is so good that you can pencil into your calculation a 10 per cent return annually on your mutual fund. Add to this strange logic the assumption that you can borrow money to invest at 10 per cent, earn an average of 8 per cent in an insurance annuity and inflation will linger at an anemic 3 per cent over the next thirty years while your plan grows to fruition. Wow! That's a lot of assumption.

I have a certain affinity for financial planners. I've still got some old business cards with that description after my name. In reality, I was a guy selling investments and insurance for ten years. That was twice as long as the average client stays invested in his mutual fund, and three times as long as the average policyholder keeps his life insurance. I have also been an investor, not always a successful one, over the past twenty-five years. I will be presumptuous enough to think that this qualifies me to make some comments on the present-day marketing of mutual funds. I will concentrate the discussion in this chapter on mutual funds for the following reasons:

1. For most investors the initial foray into the stock market is through mutual funds.

2. Most financial planning guides that have been written recently have strongly recommended investing in mutual funds as a building block to your future retirement in riches. They are also used in every positive chart, graph and illustration. We are left with the impression that for most investment needs mutual funds are the answer. Could this have something to do with the fact that the authors of such advice sell mutual funds, they are paid to speak at mutual fund presentations, and their books are distributed to mutual fund sales people?

I would like to address the premise upon which many financial plans are constructed.

Theory number 1. "We have discovered the secret to wealth: the 10 per cent solution." The idea to put aside 10 per cent of our income is not new. A reflection of our times is seen in the way in which we choose to use this 10 per cent. In the days of ancient Israel their law stated to set aside 10 per cent of their earnings to be used in worship. In more recent history, families were urged to set aside 10 per cent of their earnings to be used for charitable works in the community. Today, in this period of self-worship, we are informed of the brilliant idea of setting aside 10 per cent of our earnings to be hoarded for our exclusive use at a future time. When did financial planners come up with this piece of wisdom? From the attention given to this mantra of "save 10" you would be led to believe that this gem is a newly coined expression. In 1926 George Classon published *The Richest Man in Babylon* which gave this same advice. This little book, which is still in print, was widely distributed by banks and insurance companies in its early years. Yes, your parents and grand-parents have heard "save 10 per cent" long before you made this 'discovery'. How many retired wealthy because they heard this advice? Ask your parents. However, it helped sell a lot of books, and the banks and insurance companies were surely grateful for the efforts of their customers as they started savings plans and whole life insurance policies, clinging to the dream of retiring rich.

Theory number 2. "My mutual fund has grown by 14% annually over the last five years. Why shouldn't I expect it to average 10 per cent over the life of my financial plan?" The short answer is: "That's great! Congratulations! Now quit while your ahead." The reasons are a little more detailed. First, call up 20 of your dearest and oldest friends and relatives. Find out how many of them have received 10 per cent annually over the past 30 years in the market. You need proof; don't just have them tell you that they've done really well or their brother made a killing. If this is your future plan, you need to have proof. "But most mutual funds haven't been around for even 10 years let alone 30." That's true. Not under the names that we now recognize them. But rest assured that there have been similar schemes for as long as there's been a modern day stock market (which by the way is older than any of our friends.) It is a common fallacy to think that we are the first to discover something. The truth is that very few things have yet to be discovered, at least when it comes to making money.

It took the Dow Jones Industrials 80 years to reach 1000 points. During this time we had the greatest scientific, technical and medical advances in modern history. Of all the gadgets that we have on our list of absolute needs, how many existed in the year 1897 when the New York Stock Exchange began? Yet for all that progress the Dow moved less than 1000 points. Indeed, there were long stretches in which your mutual funds would have a negative return. For example, there was no growth from 1897 to 1917, yet the country was in full employment with the industrial revolution under full steam. The automobile and airplane were in the early stages of development and excitement. Can you imagine the frenzy today with such a stock? There was no growth from 1928 to 1948. It's true there was the '29 crash followed by the depression But can you be sure that we couldn't have a 20 year period like that again? Are we that much more clever now than then? There was no growth from 1965 to 1975. You could reason that the U.S. was embroiled in the Vietnam War, but when hasn't the U.S. been involved in some war or uprising?

Now we look at the past 20 years and the Dow has climbed from 1000 to 11000 points. Pretty amazing stuff. What has accounted for this unprecedented rise? Could it be as simple as pent-up demand spread out over 100 years, finally being released? Think of it as rowing a boat. For all the effort you put forth when you begin to row, the boat advances very slowly. Suddenly, it is being propelled ahead with very little effort. Even after we stop rowing, it continues to advance some distance. Stocks have been carried along past the historical value of what the underlying business can support. To expect more from this 20 year bull market is fantasy. As I write this, (December 2000) I am aware that there has been a pulling back from the highs. Some may feel that this represents a correction and it's time to buy. The Dow has shed 10 percent and the NASDAQ and TSE have lost substantially more. This only brings us back to the summer of 1999 levels. What will happen to mutual funds when the levels return to the more sustainable 1987 levels?

Theory number 3. "I'm into dollar cost averaging, so I want the market to come down so I can buy more." Sounds reasonable, you want to buy on sale. Agreed, but under ONE condition. What condition? Let's go through a real numbers exercise. This is not speculation. This is actual market performance. Under the formula for dollar cost averaging, at specific intervals of time you repeatedly invest an equal dollar amount. When units of your mutual fund are low, you can buy more; when the units are higher, you buy less. The object is to accumulate units, and with the gyrations of the market your price will be an average of the unit values over the life of your period of investing. You might invest every month; but, for ease of calculations, let's say you invested $1,000 at the end of every year. The year is 1986. You are 30 years old, married with 2.1 children.(The .1 child looks like your brother-in-law.) You have your expenses under control, and you begin your financial plan. Your goal is to retire at 55. With that much time ahead you feel that you can be aggressive in investing for the first 20 years. At 10 per cent return you'll have $63,000. When you reach 50 you are going to transfer your winnings into something more conservative. Follow the numbers:

Year	Dollars Invested	Unit Price	Units Bought	Total $	Total #
1986	$1000	$13.00	75	$1000	75
1987	$1000	$20.00	50	$2000	125
1988	$1000	$25.00	40	$3000	165
1989	$1000	$39.00	26	$4000	191
1990	$1000	$30.00	34	$5000	225
1991	$1000	$25.00	40	$6000	265
1992	$1000	$20.00	50	$7000	315
1993	$1000	$17.00	60	$8000	375
1994	$1000	$16.00	65	$9000	440
1995	$1000	$22.00	45	$10000	485

Year	Dollars Invested	Unit Price	Units Bought	Total $	Total #
1996	$1000	$18.00	55	$11000	540
1997	$1000	$15.00	67	$12000	607
1998	$1000	$18.00	55	$13000	662
1999	$1000	$22.00	45	$14000	707
2000	$1000	$15.00	65	$15000	772

How are you doing? You've got lots of ups and downs, just like the financial planner said there would be. You're an unusual person. You see, the average fund buyer stays in only 5 years, but you've got discipline. Fifteen years and $15,000 later, you have 772 units of your fund. The unit price is now $15.00. So your 772 units are worth $11,580 and you have 5 years to reach your $63000! Now what? Do you cut your losses and pull out now? Do you hang in and take your chances? Remember you're only 10 years from retirement and 5 years from becoming conservative. "Foul!" you cry out. " What fund performed like that?" It's the Japanese Nikkei Exchange. Look at the chart. They are not high risk penny stocks. The Nikkei Index holds the cream of Japanese commerce like Toyota, Honda, Nintendo and Sony. Now take the Nikkei Index chart and lay it along-side the Dow and TSE. Do you notice the similarities between them? Of course, there's no way of knowing whether we could have a 15 year period like the Nikkei but do you want to hang you future on it? The condition for dollar cost averaging? In order to work for you, the unit value must be higher than the

JAPAN NIKKEI

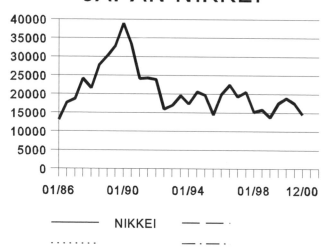

NIKKEI

U.S. DOW JONES

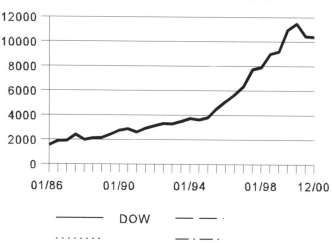

DOW

average price you paid before you cash in. In an extended bear market dollar cost averaging means you lose more every year.

Theory number 4. "I would hang in, I'm committed. I'm a Warren Buffett type. You know, the legendary investor. He holds stocks forever."

Mr. Buffett only buys into companies that he understands. He has the attitude that he may have to run the company in the future. He buys a large enough position that he has a say in the direction that the company should go. That's far different than sitting outside, looking in, and not knowing why (or even if and when) important events are taking place. There's not much fun in reading numbers. Compare this to actually having a share in the decision making. If you invest in a neighbour's farm, you can climb on the fence and watch the cattle grazing, jump down and walk over and brush the horses. You can reach down and grab a handful of earth and smell the life. You may even wander into the chicken house, reach under a startled hen and collect a dividend for breakfast. You can get another dividend just by watching the family work the farm, knowing that your investment is making a difference to their well-being. This might explain Warren Buffett's longevity in investing, but few can extract these rewards by plunking down $1,000 in a mutual fund.

In the turmoil of a plunging market, we lose sight of our initial enthusiasm. Even in good times, the average fund buyer is gone within five years. Why? As many reasons as there are investors but some are obvious:

A) market volatility : no matter how you prepare yourself, it affects you.

B) the Next Big Thing : day-trading or a real estate surge enticing your dollars.

C) circumstances change: sickness, family changes, loss of employment.

D) we only thought we were committed. One out of two marriages entered into today will fail. On average these marriages fail after only 5 years. (Sound familiar) Half of all minor children are living with only one of their natural parents. Face it: we are not a nation of committed people. Yet, we all think that we are different. We want to feel committed to our long term plans. It makes us feel responsible. Why else do we buy so many long-term warranties? My friend bought a new van on the weekend. It came with a three year warranty. He bought an additional 5 year warranty for $880. He then bought rust proofing and paint protection, both with life-time warranties. Over $2500 worth of warranties. He came over to ask me, after, if it was a good idea. I only had two questions: "What's the longest you've ever owned a vehicle?"

The response after a moment of reflection was "Two years."

My second question was harder. "Can you get your money back?"

~ ~ ~

So what do you invest in to achieve your goals? Hopefully by now you have redefined some of these goals. You now are thinking about self-respect, family and community. We're thinking about a happy retirement but also a happy journey to that retirement. It's important to have a cushion to provide for the unknown. Before you embark on any long term financial planning you should have sufficient savings to cover your living costs for three to six months. If you find yourself in a temporary earning blip, where you are looking at a greater tax bill than usual, stick this emergency fund in a registered account to avoid the tax consequences.

DO NOT UNDER ANY CIRCUMSTANCES ATTEMPT TO KEEP AN RRSP UNTIL AGE 65. IT CAN CAUSE SERIOUS INJURY OR DEATH TO YOUR FINANCIAL WELL BEING.

Like a manufacturer's warning label on a potentially dangerous toy or instrument this warning should be issued in a prospectus with every savings plan registered with Revenue Canada. Over the years I have had many RRSPs and at this time I have none. I use them purely as an instrument to avoid paying taxes. Not tax deferral, tax avoidance. Let me explain. Some years I may earn $30,000. That hurts. It means I pay tax. Other years I earn $15,000. That hurts. I need more than that to live. In the years that I earn too much income, I buy an RRSP. Large enough to ensure I pay very little tax. The government lets you defer your RRSP contributions for up to 7 years, so I always have enough room to contribute. In the years that I earn below what I need, I withdraw the RRSP. Large enough to bring my income to the tax-paying threshold. If you do not have any lean years at present make sure you do before you begin drawing any pension. Let me illustrate what goes wrong with your financial plan when you have too much in an RRSP at age 65. Let us imagine that you are 35 years old and married. Your financial advisor has praised the value of the RRSP, Revenue Canada's gift to mankind. You are told that in your present tax bracket, for every $1,000 you contribute, (naturally to the investment which he/she is selling) you will save $400, in this year's taxes. Further, this $1,000 will grow inside the shelter unencumbered by annual taxes on the gain. This is good—or is it?

Okay, you know the routine. Sit down on Free Parking and slowly think of all the consequences. Let me tell you a little more about you. You have a mortgage on your house for $80,000 at 8 percent. You have a car loan of $12,000 at 10 per cent. You plan on borrowing $5,000 for an RRSP. The bank will lend you the money for 8 per cent if you put your RRSP with them; otherwise it will be a loan at 10 per cent. The stock market has you nervous (me too), so you take the bank's offer and stick your money in a registered GIC for 5 years at 6 per cent. You claim your $2,000 refund cheque from Revenue Canada and shrewdly apply it to your loan. You diligently make monthly payments of $275 a month for 12 months and retire the $3,000 balance. You have paid $250 interest to the bank. This interest paid would otherwise have been paid on your mortgage. We therefore will calculate this accumulating at 8 per cent. Are you happy with this scenario? Okay, we're having so much fun let's repeat this same scene each year until you are 65 and watch what happens.

Age	DEPOSIT	INTEREST Paid	Earned	Total RRSP
35	$5,000	$250	$300	$5,300
36	$10,000	$562	$920	$10,920
37	$15,000	$876	$1875	$16,875
38	$20,000	$1216	$2630	$22,630
39	$25,000	$1584	$4875	$29,875
40	$30,000	$1980	$6970	$36,970
41	$35,000	$2409	$9485	$44,485
42	$40,000	$2872	$12455	$52,455
43	$45,000	$3371	$15905	$60,905
45	$55,000	$4494	$24,350	$79,350
50	$80,000	$8187	$56,065	$136,065
55	$105,000	$13614	$106,960	$211,960
60	$130,000	$21587	$180,530	$313,530
65	$155,000	$33,303	$294,450	$449,450

Well look at you. You've really done it. Methodically saving over all these years and it's just like in the brochures. Almost half a million. What else has happened over the last 30 years? The house is paid off. You had three children since we last spoke. They're all gone with families of their own. You and your wife are in great health, you're looking forward to your golden years. You've had regular visits from financial advisors over the years. Your current one is talking life insurance. You don't need the protection, but your financial planner has convinced you that the thought of paying all the tax to the government when you both die is too much to bear. You settle on a policy on your wife for $250,000. It's term 100 which is the least expensive policy that will last forever. If you die first the RRSPs will be rolled over to your wife without triggering the tax. When your wife dies the policy will pay most of the tax due on the RRSPs. The premium is $3,500 per year. You wince at the cost, but by now you are caught up in the game of out-foxing the tax man. Your advisor even suggests that the kids can pay the premium, since they stand to benefit from the estate. You may like the idea, but do you know any children with kids of their own in school who have an extra $3,500 a year to invest in their parents' death? You hesitate, and your advisor (who has suddenly become a life insurance salesman) turns pale. We'll talk more about his reaction in the next chapter; but for now let's assume that he prevails and you buy the policy. Now it's time to start reaping the benefits. You set up a RRIF and slowly begin collapsing your RRSPs. You agree to $40,000 a year from your RRSP. That's a little more than the interest being earned but you must use it all before you die. You can expect a further $15,000 a year from Canada Pension. The basic exemption for seniors is now $16,000. One other thing has happened. Just as your original financial planner predicted, the government has wiped out the Old Age Security for anyone in your income bracket. For the low-income senior, it is now $11,000 per year. It has escalated to this amount in keeping with inflation indexing that the government set up. Your neighbour and his wife qualify. Like you they recently sold their home and took the proceeds and bought a condominium. But unlike you, they only have Canada Pension and OAS. You wonder how they are getting by with no RRSPs. Let's be nosey and look.

Family Income	Taxes	Insurance Premiums	Your's To spend	Neighbour's To spend
$55,000	$11,000	$3,500	$40,500	$35,000

You and your wife have $5,500 more a year to spend then does your neighbour. Before you bring out the champagne, think what it cost you. You deposited $155,000 and you paid further interest charges that accumulated to $33,000. You did save $2,000 a year in taxes so you were only out of pocket $126,000. What did your neighbour do with his extra $3,250 per year while you were carefully putting yours in the RRSP? He took time off work. When you were working evenings, he was reading bed-time stories to his twins. When you were away on business trips, he was camping with the family. When you were filing reports to head office, he was at Parent-Teacher interviews. When you were planning for your golden years, he was enjoying his golden years—his family's golden years.

Even from a purely financial aspect, you have made a poor investment. You have spent out of pocket $126,000. Had you put that $3,000 a year on your mortgage or car loan imagine how much faster you would have retired these loans and retired yourself. You have forfeited the OAS benefit and any other income related goodies that may have come along in the thirty years since you began your plan. For what? To have an extra $5,500 a year to spend. It will take you almost twenty-three years (not accounting for interest) to get your $126,000 back at $5,500 per year. By then you and your wife will be in your mid-eighties. Will you have many years left to enjoy the extra income? If you were saving all that money to give to your kids to show you love them, there are better ways that are a lot more fun. If this is your RRSP, I'm sorry to ruin your day. But there is one bright spot. It may not be too late. It may take radical surgery; but, like the cure for flesh-eating disease, it may be your only reasonable option. I know of a couple who realized the tax consequences of reaching age 65 with their RRSPs still growing strong. They made a decision to retire at age 55. They began collapsing their RRSPs and living off the proceeds with a view to having none left by 65. They don't want to lose the government benefits that are in store.

"But my neighbours' well-being is contingent on there being Old Age Security in 30 years time. How can you trust your future to the care of the government?" To some degree, we are all at the mercy of governments. Could they eliminate all social programs? Yes. Could they nationalize all financial institutions and seize the assets of the wealthy? Yes. Some governments in our lifetime have done just that. My point is: it's fruitless to speculate about what may or may-not happen. You plan for what you know—for what is in place now. What makes me so sure that these programs will exist (and probably be expanded)? Because the government will be able to afford it. Where will they get the money? From you, my soon-to-be-wealthy friend. As you are forced to liquidate your RRSPs, you will be taxed on all withdrawals. The tax-deferral you received when you contributed to your RRSP will be small in comparison to the taxes paid when it is collapsed. The government has assured itself of future revenue. They have encouraged you to plant your kernel of grain. They have patiently watched as you fed and watered it. Now they sit ready to reap! Not only will you be a willing tax payer with few deductions, you will be so self-sufficient that future politicians will feel no regret in clawing back your portion of senior's programs. Without your future generous donations, I would be concerned about the government's ability to care for we low-income seniors. For this I thank-you, kind sir.

Most people work five days a week at jobs that they don't particularly like, so they can spend two days a week with people they love. They work forty-five years so they can retire for ten or fifteen years. What's wrong with this picture? With proper planning, and controlling our spending habits, we could reverse those figures in our favour.

Now look at the long term. Sit on Free Parking, look at your goals and priorities and consider these suggestions: Instead of Government Bonds chose Family Bonds. Blood may be thicker than water, but if it's not nurtured it can get somewhat anemic.

Successful investing in family life takes planning and work, but neglect it at your peril. The benefits of a close, happy family are obvious but consider the ramifications of family break-up to your financial well-being. Lawyers for you and your spouse, psychiatrists for any children. Try factoring those costs into your retirement equation. If bonding is not your strong point, practice talking to the family pet until you can carry on a conversation without wishing you were at work.

Instead of GICs, invest in KIDs. In past civilizations, and a few current ones, children were the retirement savings plan. If you had no children to care for you in your old age, you were destitute with no means of support. This being so, how diligent do you suppose the parents would be to give their offspring the very best of training? I'm not talking about sending them off to day-care until they can be sent to boarding school before they're sent to university. I'm talking about one-on-one training with your child, YOU teaching him life skills for earning a living, interacting with others and having a defined sense of morality and justice. He can't learn it from his peers and certainly not from television or video games. In fact, exposing children to much of what is now loosely termed as entertainment is putting this valuable investment at risk. Before we invest in mutual funds we examine the fund manager's credentials and track record. We owe it to our children to examine their associates just as carefully, whether they be in the classroom, the mall or on television. This is not just philosophy on child rearing. This is practical financial planning. Your children will either grow up to be an asset to your reputation and financial well-being or they will be a liability. Like most investments, there are no guarantees. But you owe it to both your family and your financial plan to anticipate the risks and work to eliminate them where possible. Remember Mr. Jackson's son, Carl, from Chapter two?

Instead of mutual funds, invest in mutual respect. It appears to me that we have become focused on self-fulfillment. Everyone wants to be a self-made man. Not content with being comfortable with our lot in life we want it all. Sometimes it involves taking it from someone else. Executives get bonuses for cutting expenses, which often involve cutting jobs. We refer to it as down-sizing and the financial community embraces it. The stock market rewards investors who buy into such a company. The banks praise its leadership. It's all so clinically sanitary—like "ethnic cleansing". Everyone is happy, except the employees, and they are considered as excessive inventory that can always be re-ordered at a future date, if necessary. Employees strike back. They steal property from their employers. They treat loyalty like a social disease, to be inoculated against with large doses of business-bashing. They abscond with their time and energy, that their employer has paid for, by slacking off on the job or calling in "sick". There was a time when caring employers cared for grateful employees. If an employee was ill, he could rest at home and still receive his salary. More and more employees demand a designated amount of sick-days every year regardless of their health. Who thinks up these schemes? You take a kind and gentle hand, extended in compassion, and twist it into a gnarled stick and use it to beat its owner.

Gambling is a global addiction with governments feeding off the victims like back alley crack dealers. Lotteries continue to be a growth industry and now governments have become the latest casualties, addicted to the easy money. Schools and hospitals rely on the proceeds of lotteries which a few years ago was a criminal activity. Gamblers form long lines when the purse climbs into the multimillions, as if a mere million is no longer of interest. The Canadian government adds to the lure of gambling by declaring it a tax-free winning. What lesson does this teach society when we tax the labour of citizens but reward gambling by declaring it a tax-free zone? Lotteries are essentially the taking of small amounts of money from our neighbours so that we might have it all. Tell me how this builds respect for our fellows. There was a time when neighbours looked out for one another, now they look in fear at one another. We keep our possessions locked up and out of sight because there is no mutual respect for life or property. We are reluctant to donate our resources or time to charities because we fear being exploited. Organizations that were set up to assist the vulnerable are themselves becoming vulnerable, open to lawsuits and unseemly accusations. Unfortunately, sometimes the accusations are true. We could all do with a large investment in mutual respect.

"What's in it for me?" you ask.

This is one investment that may not pay off in terms of take-home dollars to spend as you wish. But there are real benefits.

You can wake up in the morning, look yourself in the mirror, and be pleased with what you have become. Not a self-made individual, but something greater.   An important person in the lives of others. A companion to your wife with time to share. A mentor and protector to your children, taking time to recognize potential dangers and stepping in to ward off calamity. A friend and real neighbour in the community who makes a difference to the quality of life. You will not change the world, but you just may help someone as you journey along life's path. You will know that you invested; you tried. And whether you see the tangible results in others or not, you will have something that the changing economic climate can never erode. Not net-worth, but self-worth.

Do you really want to retire to a gated community with armed guards and twenty-four hour surveillance cameras? Wealthy individuals are spending   large amounts of their precious savings to reside in these communities. There was a time when we would give lawyers large amounts to keep us out of communities that had armed guards and walls topped with razor-wire. Many have fled to Canada as a safe haven from intruders and violence. But here, too, individuals keep to themselves lest they divulge some piece of information that makes them a target. In the rural areas, guard-dogs are not kept as status symbols but as reminders that we live in a land of no mutual respect.

When companies want to attract investors, they persuade respected analysts to examine them and issue buy recommendations. Too bad that we couldn't do the same for basic human qualities like respect, honesty, empathy, humility and kindness. We could set up rating firms like "Standards & Free" or "Good-man & Sons". If they issued a 'strong buy' on Family and an 'avoid' on Avarice would we listen?

6

FINANCIAL
FABLES
PART 2—INSURANCE

"Dividend—A partial repayment
of an overpayment." —
Glossary of Life Insurance terms

My chances to succeed looked good. I had passed the
aptitude test and the provincial examination, I had paid my ten
dollars for the licence, and less than one month after meeting
the sales manager, I was a financial planner. Then I came
across this definition for an insurance dividend in the recesses
of a training manual. It altered my attitude toward this industry.
I began questioning the integrity of the products and the people
involved in management and sales. I still do. I knew what a
stock dividend was, but this definition was unique to this
business. In my experience, you invested in a company that you
believed in and when it became profitable the company
rewarded the investors with a dividend or portion of the

profits. But this was different. This was life insurance. I visualize it this way: the box of soap costs $3. In that price is all the components such as raw materials, wages, factories, marketing and profit. The manufacturer puts another label on the box. He calls it "participating soap" and charges $5. You pay an extra $2 for every box you buy, but if the company makes a profit they will give you some of that extra $2 back and call it a dividend. How much? You don't know—nobody does. In good years you might get 20 cents back for every box of soap you bought. But don't stop buying the soap or you'll be disqualified.

Now you may be asking, "Why not just pay $3 for the soap? Why pay an extra $2 for the opportunity to get back 20 cents?" You would ask that question. You and thousands of others, and that's why no one ever tries this trick with soap. You know what a box of soap costs. You can compare the price of the same brand at various stores across town. You know what brand works best for you and which is the most cost effective.

Life insurance is a horse of a different colour. I'm not against life insurance. I sold it for ten years and still carry a policy on my life, but I've always been uncomfortable with the way the product was—and continues to be—sold. I know that making such a broad statement does not account for the individuals who are doing a first rate job of looking after their clients. In my ten years, I met about a half- dozen such people. They were not industry leaders. They made a modest living, but I'm sure they slept well.

To get an overview of the life insurance buying process,

let's return to one of our couples, the Rairries, and listen in on their evening with two agents. This account is reconstructed from numerous selling experiences related in the industry. It is the way agents are trained. The time period is just after Adam starts selling at Barton Brothers. The Rairries have just moved into their new apartment. One of Adam's former co-workers, Larry, has recently started selling insurance.

~ ~ ~

"Honey, don't forget, Larry and his manager are stopping by after supper."

"Really, Adam, I don't know why you agreed to this. You know we can't afford any more expenses. It's not my idea of a fun evening."

"Oh, it won't be so bad. Larry's a nice guy. We aren't going to buy anything. Larry said he has to take his manager to see a number of his friends and relatives. He's just going to use us to give Larry some sales experience. We'll just go through the process, tell him thanks—but no thanks—and that's it. It'll probably take an hour at most. I'll help clean up. They will be here in 45 minutes."

Right on time Larry and his manager, Ted Brock, arrive and after a few minutes of remarks about the weather, 'what a lovely apartment' and 'such a bright child', the conversation is directed to the matter at hand.

"Adam, as you know, Larry has recently been licensed with Vancouver Life to act as an agent. One of the training steps we at Vancouver Life take is to assist new agents with a number of interviews with close friends and successful acquaintances. Larry tells me that you're not only a close friend, but a very successful one."

"I'm not there yet, but I do enjoy selling at Bartons." Adam also enjoyed hearing words of praise. They might not be 100 per cent sincere, but he would accept them anyway.

"I want to put you at ease, Adam. Larry and I are here only to assist you and Nancy in planning your future. Once we have an idea about your goals for the future, we can make some suggestions as to how you can achieve these goals. Don't worry. I get paid a salary from Vancouver Life as a manager. Larry is getting a training allowance. There's no pressure on you to buy, but if you decide at some point in the future that you need insurance or investments, we at Vancouver Life would like you to consider us. Is that fair, Adam?" Adam had time to nod in approval before Ted continued, "Once you've seen the way we work I know that you'll be impressed. Even if you have no needs at present, I'm sure you'll want to tell some of your friends about our service. Now, let's begin."

On cue, Larry pulled out three official looking folders from his new attache. On the cover was inscribed in embossed lettering: YOUR FINANCIAL PLAN. Larry took out a gold coloured pen and passed it to Nancy and asked her to date her personal plan. It was suggested that they would discuss each of the areas and Nancy could fill in the numbers on her copy and it could be their's to keep.

The first page was a simple budget. How much did they earn and what did they spend? Adam had just come off a good month and he was proud to see the numbers on the page. The calculations showed a healthy margin of unused income. Ted smiled.

The next page was a balance sheet. What assets did they have and what did they owe? Like most young couples, their assets and liabilities pretty well evened out. Ted congratulated them on not owing much money. He commented on the fact that it showed them to be responsible people.

On the top of the third page Ted drew three stick people, one smaller than the others. This was Adam, Nancy (the one with long hair) and little Sarah. "Now don't be alarmed, Nancy, but what happens if I do this?" and he drew a large X through the drawing of Adam. "If something was to happen to you, Adam, what would you want to happen to Nancy and Sarah?" His tone was low, almost sympathetic for the bereaved.

"Well, I want the best for them."

Ted beamed like a proud father. "I just knew you'd feel that way. You're a responsible person, that's a rare quality today. Let's see how we can make sure that you get what you want, Adam. On this page we are going to fill it in with the numbers needed to look after your family if you were gone. First there are some expenses to deal with. Funerals and last expenses can be about $5,000. The experts say you should plan on your wife having about six months salary on hand for emergencies and adjusting to life without you. Based on last months income, that's another $14,000. And of course, you'll want to set aside money for Sarah—for her future education."

Nancy interrupted. "Future education? You mean university? She's only two!"

"I know," Ted was undaunted, "you'd be surprised how fast the time goes. And besides, the sooner money is set aside, the more time it has to grow. Can you imagine the cost for university in 18 years? You need about $15,000 for a four year program in today's dollars.

"These are some of the immediate concerns. Now, Adam, do you think your wife and child will need more money, less money or about the same amount every month to maintain their current life-style?"

"I guess most of the costs would be about the same."

"You're right. The experts tell us that costs continue at the same rate. We can come up with that money in two ways. One is to work every day for it. The other way is like the rich do. They have money work for them. Which would you prefer for your family, Adam? Send your wife out to work —remember little Sarah—or have enough money invested to provide them with a monthly income?"

"Wouldn't Nancy just remarry?"

"Where could she ever find another man like you?"
Ted liked using that line. It always got a laugh, especially from the wife. "All joking aside, the experts say that very few women remarry. Especially those with young children."

"When you put it that way; I'd like Nancy to have enough money so she didn't have to work.... unless she wanted to after Sarah was older."

"Very responsible, Adam. So how much money are we talking about, do you think?"

"I don't know. Sounds like a lot. What about Canada Pension. Isn't there money in there for survivors?"

"I can see that you've done your homework, Adam. Most people wouldn't know that until I tell them. Yes, between Nancy and Sarah, Canada Pension will pay about $400 per month, if it is still around. And Larry says you have $20,000 of insurance at work, but most experts say you can't count on group insurance. The insurance company or Barton Brothers could drop the insurance without notice. Here's how we calculate the amount of insurance you need. You add up the immediate needs and that comes to, uh, $34,000. Now we take the $2200 a month that you say your family will need and subtract the $400 from Canada Pension, if it hasn't gone broke, leaving $1800 a month. If we figure your investment earns 8 percent, it would take about $260,000 to earn $1800 every month. Add the other $34,000 and you need almost $300,000."

"That much! I can't afford to die."

"It's always a shock to look at the numbers, and no one expects you to load up with all that protection at once. But what if I showed you a way to start building a secure future for Nancy and Sarah. Would you be interested?"

"Sure....I guess."

"Adam, you've got two things going for you. You're young and so the insurance is cheap at your age. And you've got time on your side. By getting into a program today, you can have your protection grow while keeping the costs low. Let's see. Your budget shows you have an extra $80 every month. What if I showed you how you could protect your family and make that money grow at the same time? Sound good to you, Adam?" Ted was nodding his head in assumed consent. Adam unconsciously nodded his head in unison.

Ted flipped open the rate manual; Larry got out his copy and tried best to follow. "This is our 'executive life' policy, Adam. It's been designed for up and comers like you. At your age, you can have $50,000 in this policy for only $65 per month, and we can add on an additional $100,000 of term or temporary insurance for another $15. Now watch how this executive life grows. By reinvesting the dividends to increase your protection, in 20 years this policy grows from $50,000 to almost $130,000. The best part is that you are still only depositing $60 per month. Fantastic! And look at this. Nancy, you don't want to think about Adam dying. Am I right?" Ted has Nancy nodding now. "What happens when you're ready to put your feet up at age 65? You both want to enjoy the good life. Now your policy pays $270,000 at death, or—and I like this part—you cash it in and take out $63,000. You've got back twice as much as you deposited. Can you believe it! I've seen a lot of programs and there's nothing like it. Now to get this plan working for you, I'll need your social insurance number, Adam."

"Can we back up for a minute, Ted?" You said the first $50,000 was $65 per month and then the next $100,000 was only $15. Why?"

"Good question. The $65 is a deposit on the executive plan. As you can see you get all of that money back, and then some. It's like putting a down payment on a house and watching it go up in value. The $100,000 is temporary insurance. You're just renting the protection every month for $15. The money's gone, there's no investment. When you're starting out you need the extra protection. Once your executive life grows, you can stop renting. Any other questions before we go ahead?"

"I guess not. But $80 a month, that's a big commitment. What do you think, Nancy? It sounds pretty good."

"I think we should talk it over for a few days." Nancy was getting a headache. Somehow the one hour had grown to three hours.

"It's wise to think financial matters over." Ted began, choosing his words carefully. "If there's any questions, you should have them answered before you proceed. Adam, do you agree with the numbers that Nancy wrote down? The amount of money your family needs to be properly cared for?" Ted nodded and Adam reciprocated. "Do you understand the way we calculated the amount of insurance that would look after this responsibility?" The nodding continued like a silent ritual. "Do you see the value of owning an investment that provides for your family now and in the future?" At this point Ted paused. The application was on the table, his pen was ready. He silently counted, pacing the time for the next move. Most in Adam's position would consent at this point. What was holding him back?

"We could call you in the morning." Nancy offered.

"Larry," Ted said as he turned to his silent partner, "this reminds me of Gregory Alcot. Did I ever tell you about him. He was a friend of mine. I had just got into the insurance business. He had a young family, like yours, Adam. Anyway, I talked to him about insurance, and he was ready to start. But he hesitated, and I didn't like to push. I hate pushy salesmen; don't you Adam? We agreed to fill out the paper work the next day over lunch and I left. The next morning on the way to work he was in an accident and died. I think about him everyday. If I would have just done my job a little better, his wife wouldn't be working at a fast food joint now." Ted's last words were muffled and his eyes were glazed. It was all he could do to finish the story.

"I guess it could happen anytime." Adam conceded as he reached in his wallet and retrieved his Social Insurance Card. "I'm going to need it sooner or later. Why take a chance?"

The forms were completed, a cheque for the first month's payment and authorization for monthly withdrawals were signed. It was time to leave. Ted and Larry said quick good-byes, all the while congratulating the Rairries on their wise decision. They shook hands. Ted and Larry walked to the car. Adam and Nancy locked the door and walked to the bedroom. It was midnight.

Larry and Ted reviewed the events of the evening as Ted drove Larry home. It had been a good night. They would split the commission. 100 percent of the first year's payments on the executive life and 50 percent for the term. $840—$420 each. Ted would get another $250 override and bonus, but there was no need to burden Larry with all the details. Ted kept his agents on a need-to-know basis. Larry didn't need to know. Larry was standing outside his house with the car door still open when he turned back to console Ted.

"I'm sorry about your friend Gregory. I didn't know. Were you really good friends?"

"The best friend an insurance agent ever had." Ted smiled and headed for home.

Have you had a visit from Ted and Larry? At some point in our life we will. It may only be one of them, but if all goes according to the life insurance company's plan you will be the proud owner of an insurance policy. Did you make a good purchase? Perhaps. Did you make a wise investment? Perhaps. Let's examine what took place at the Rairries, and maybe you can answer the previous questions for yourself.

Why did Ted and Larry get an opportunity to sell life insurance to the Rairries? It is well known in consumer sales organizations that the easiest sales are made to friends and relatives. It is not without reason that candidates for sales jobs are queried about their personal contacts. It would be much more difficult for Ted to get an appointment with the Rairries than for Larry to do so. The quickest and easiest way for Ted to sell to Adam is for Ted to recruit Larry. If Larry fails in his new career, as four out of five do, Ted has still made money selling to Larry's contacts.

Rule number one: Be wary of buying life insurance from a friend or relative who is new to the business.

When Larry brought out the fact finding forms, Adam and Nancy were impressed with the thoroughness of this process. Here was a company that was interested in knowing their clients. The agents were not just there to sell a product off the shelf. A needs analysis was to be done to determine what was in the best interests of the Rairries. Adam and Nancy were to calculate for themselves their present needs and to chart the course for the future. It was to be their plan. No two would be alike. Or would they?

How long do you think the agents would have stayed if the first page had revealed that the Rairries had no money available for life insurance? When Ted talked about future expenses, he was frequently quoting 'experts'. He suggested that the experts put the price of funerals at $5,000. It's true you could spend that much, but where there is a memorial society, a simple service is under $1500 and Canada Pension pays up to $2500 for this expense. Many "financial planners" speak of putting aside funds for the children's university education. Nancy questioned the validity of this and rightly so. Aren't we making enough assumptions, with the prediction of imminent death, without trying to forecast the future for infants? It would be just as reasonable to conclude that the child would be gifted with great intelligence and receive generous scholarships to pay her way.

Rule number two: Know the benefits provided by government programs and consider them an asset. Do not discount them for they will most likely be around longer than your private insurance or your agent.

The group insurance that Adam had at work was dismissed as having no merit. It was blamed on the 'experts' who had declared that since one does not control the master group policy, the group insurance is not reliable. Of course the truth is that group coverage remains in force with greater consistency than does the personal policy that the agents are about to recommend. Rather than conclude that this insurance is of no value, Adam would have been wise to inquire if he could purchase additional coverage at work if the rates were acceptable.

Rule number three: Group insurance is a valuable asset and can provide some or even all of your insurance needs.

Adam is led to believe that his family needs his highest month's earnings to be comfortable. In reality, they had been comfortable on much less a year earlier. A further assumption is made that this monthly income will be needed indefinitely, and therefore sufficient capital must be raised to generate enough interest to live forever. Some planners will even go further and build an increasing stream of income to offset future inflation. These escalating figures have the desired effect on Adam. He feels vulnerable. He suspects that he has been placing the security of his family at risk. Overwhelmed by the $300,000 figure, he is suddenly at ease with the suggestion of starting at $150,000. Like a good negotiator, Ted has set the initial figure high. He can always come down.

Ted returns to the monthly cash available in the budget. It is the primary reason for the needs analysis. Once he knows how much money he can tap the Rairries for, the rest of the form is redundant. If Ted was only concerned about Adam's family and really believed there was a need for $300,000 of life insurance, a ten year term policy could have been purchased for under $30 per month. This would have more than satisfied Adam's needs. Ted was thinking about Ted's needs. People who realize a need will buy term insurance. It makes sense. You pay a premium for a specific amount of protection. Executive Life, or whatever the popular name today is for a non-term product, needs to be sold. An agent is required to use euphemisms to hide the product. Ted talks about re-investing dividends like you were buying shares of Bell Canada. He doesn't say that you have to pay $65 a month but rather you are depositing this money, like it is a guaranteed bank account. He paints a scene of a full rich retirement, thanks to your wise selection. He tosses out future numbers, declaring that you've been protected and have doubled your money in the process. There is no mention that these figures will not be guaranteed in the policy. Just more assumptions. Mind you, life insurance companies are much more selective about predictions for future returns since a number of them have been successfully sued by disgruntled policyholders when these predictions failed to materialized. Whole life policies are said to be owned, giving us a sense of pride. Indeed Ted uses the common comparison to real estate. Term insurance is disparagingly described as just renting—throwing away your money. Not true. You are buying something. Buying protection and peace of mind.

Ted has successfully pulled a "bait-and-switch" maneuvre

on the Rairries. In identifying the need for insurance, Ted has described the uncertainty of life. You need to have life insurance because your wife could be widowed tomorrow. This is true, therefore a genuine need for insurance. Adam or Ted or anyone else for that matter could die tomorrow or next week and thus there is a need. Adam has been lured by the bait of his own mortality. The selling part comes into play by the sudden disappearance of Adam's body on a slab, only to reappear relaxed, enjoying retirement with his wife.

Retirement is a much more pleasant concept to dwell upon than death. We cannot blame Adam or his wife for gravitating in this direction. But what about Ted? His motives are more mercenary. A $300,000 term insurance policy that costs $350 a year will yield commissions to the salesman of about $180 the first year and $35 a year for the next several years. But remember the prize for the policy sold to the Rairries. The winnings are almost five times as high in the first year and at least double thereafter. So what? Many salesman go for the higher commission. Is that not the incentive behind this type of compensation? Why should we expect anything different from life insurance agents?

We aren't talking about a used car that's been sitting on the dealer's lot for so long that the salesman is paid a bonus to flog it to the next customer. The worst that happens in this scenario, is you get stuck with a lemon that drains your bank balance until you unload it. What is the worst that could happen to the Rairries? They pay the $80 and Ted is right! Adam does die the next day. "Wonderful!" you exclaim. "Ted's a hero. He's rescued Adam's widow and infant daughter from a life of poverty."

No. Ted's a bum. He's robbed Adam's family of half a million dollars. That's the extra insurance $80 would have bought had they purchased term. They didn't need that much coverage. However, Ted had coaxed them into believing they needed at least $300,000. If this figure was accurate, given the money available, Adam should have bought at least this amount. If he was intent on taking the full $80, the very least Ted could have done was given Adam the full amount of coverage that his money would buy—about $700,000.

Seldom do we witness the worst case scenarios. The used car we buy siphons off only half of our resources. We dump it at the first opportunity and chalk it up to experience. The insurance policy we pay too much for is stuffed in a drawer and forgotten about. The payments silently sneak their way out of our bank account until we stub our toe on life's financial walkway. In Adam's case it happens when his income evaporates as the economy shrivels. The bank returns the authorized payment unpaid from insufficient funds. The bank charges Adam $20 for this kindness. Larry, his agent, appears for the first time since the night of the sale, and attempts to recover the defaulted payment and the next one that is almost due. Adam manages to come up with the money, but six months later when the scene is repeated, Adam admits defeat and the policy lapses. Larry doesn't come by this time. It's not just the policy that's lapsed, it's also Adam's agent. He's trying his hand at selling encyclopedias. Ted makes a phone call, but it's brief. He knows better than to spend too much time on lapses. Besides, the policy has been in force long enough. He won't have to pay back any commissions. What about Vancouver Life? They would have preferred the policy continue, at least for a few more years. But don't feel bad for them. They recovered their underwriting costs after two years. The policy was in force for almost three years, about a year less than average. It is surreal to speak of cash values and future dividends at age 65 when the average life of a life insurance policy is under four years. Is it any wonder that many life insurance agents never deliver a death benefit?

Ted has done alright on the policy. Vancouver Life has suffered no ill effects. What about Adam and Nancy? By the time the last payment had been squeezed out of their bank account, the policy had been in force for 33 months. They had paid $2640. During that time, Adam had received $150,000 worth of life insurance coverage valued at about $640. What happened to the other $2,000? There was a few dollars in dividends that had accumulated in the policy reserve, which was quickly used in extending the life of the policy another two months after Adam stopped paying. For an explanation about the whereabouts of the remaining "deposits" you'll have to look at Ted's paycheque. Of course, there are layers of management above Ted which all need to be fed.

As for Adam and his family, they have been educated as to the very real need for insurance. Adam feels the loss of this protection when the policy expires. But the other household expenses are too demanding. With his current income, the $80 is beyond his ability to pay. For years to come, whenever the subject of life insurance is introduced, Adam reflects on his experience and laments that it is just too expensive. His self-esteem is lower than his bank balance as he contemplates the future for his wife and daughter if he should die. He says a quiet prayer for protection. Nancy prefers not to think of the consequences.

Rule number four: Let the buyer beware. Question what "the experts" say about your financial needs. Know what the consequences are if you change your plans in ten years, in five years or next week. If numbers are discussed, ask if they are guaranteed and if they will be written in the policy.

Let's imagine that Adam and Nancy had been visited by a more ethical agent. The needs analysis took into account Adam's group insurance and the Canada Pension Plan death benefit and the survivor and orphan benefit. A realistic income needs was determined for a defined period of time. It was decided that $100,000 of life insurance was required. The agent then calculated the rate for a ten year renewable term to be $150 per year and that's what the Rairries bought. They might even have added a rider on Nancy's life for $50,000 for an additional premium of $50. They pay it once a year and it's out of the way.

The next two years when Adam is experiencing a cash crunch, he is not looking at $1,000 a year, but $200. Will he have trouble making the $200 payment? Sure, but he'll do it. It's much more manageable. The protection continues, and Adam and Nancy are secure, both financially and emotionally.

There is a trade-off for this happy ending. Ted and Larry make less money—in the short term. However, this new ethical Ted is now a true insurance planner to Adam. Adam willingly refers others to Ted, knowing that they will be conscientiously cared for. Ted doesn't need to resort to sales tricks and clever manipulation to win over his clients. He might even feel better about his profession as he recruits others.

Remember our couple in the last chapter with the half million tucked away in an RRSP? They are the next target for many seasoned insurance agents. They have the income to pay substantial premiums and they can be persuaded to believe that they have an insurance need. Oh, nothing as basic as providing a living for a bereaved spouse or orphans. No, much more compelling! The agent draws close and in a low voice suggest a scheme to thwart the tax-man. Who could resist such an idea? Finally, a way to beat Revenue Canada! Have the insurance company pay the taxes. This way, you get to keep your estate in tact.

Wait a minute! Step back and think. The insurance company isn't paying Revenue Canada. You are! In fact you are not only paying Revenue Canada, but the insurance company and the agent. It's your money. You pay the insurance premiums. If the insurance company didn't think they could cover all of their costs and still make a profit, they wouldn't sell you the policy. When we have a young family and little in the way of assets, it is advisable to provide for them in the unlikely event of our death. We can't afford to take the risk. And so, for a premium the insurance company assumes the risk. But what motivates us to buy a policy to pay taxes due on an RRSP at our death? The RRSP has filled its purpose. Remember, it's for our retirement. There's not much retirement left at death. If it is collapsed at this point and tax is paid, is there a problem with that? You **will** pay the tax. Will it come from the proceeds of a life insurance policy or from the money that you saved by not buying the policy? It's your choice.

Of course there may be real needs for life insurance in our senior years. Perhaps there are assets that will attract capital gains tax or recaptured tax at our death and there will not be sufficient cash to pay the tax. It may be an asset such as a family business that we desire to continue after our death; perhaps a sum of cash to buy out the heirs of a deceased partner.

Rule number five: Life insurance companies are in business to make money. I wouldn't want it any other way. If they continually lost money, they would be broke before they could pay my family if they have a claim. But consider this fact before you buy a policy: the odds are in the company's favour. Only insure a life when the financial loss at death will be greater than you are able to accept. If the agent has to create a need, you probably don't need it...or him.

One further point could be made about life insurance. Many agents believe in the principle of permanent insurance. They reason from two directions. First there are those that state that it is a forced savings plan. They agree that it doesn't give a good return and penalizes severely those who drop out. However, they rationalize that this penalty keeps the customer in the program and he ends up with some money that he never would have without this plan. My experience is that if the customer is sold a poor product, sooner or later he will discover this and stop paying and lose his money. The sooner the better. Deceiving someone to buy a product that we think is "for their own good"is ethically wrong.

Then there are those who blame the customer for losing money. They state that the long term benefits of the policy were never realized because the customer canceled the policy before maturity. They maintain that had the policy been allowed to continue, the customer would have been better served. They further warn of the dire consequences of getting rid of the permanent insurance. How will I be able to pay the premiums of my term insurance when the rates skyrocket as I advance in years? Let me show you how I manage to pay. When I canceled my permanent insurance, I bought 5 year term for $200 for $100,000 of coverage. At renewal, 5 years later, I was older but the rates had surrendered to competition and I now paid $200 for $150,000. At the next renewal, I was able to buy $100,000 of 10 year term for $300 annually. I no longer need as much insurance. My family is getting smaller and so is my mortgage. When this term is ready for renewal, I may not need any coverage. If I do, it is guaranteed to cost no more than $700 per year for the next 10 years. $700 is less than my permanent insurance was costing over 20 years ago.

But what if I would have kept my policy? What of the cash value benefits and dividends? During the years I worked in the life insurance industry, I had the opportunity to witness the life cycle of an insurance policy. While the majority expired within three or four years, there were some very loyal customers who had diligently paid premiums for decades. How did they fare? One in particular stuck in my mind as a poignant testimony to the need to consider life insurance as an expense.

In a typical life insurance office there are numerous orphan policyholders. These are customers who no longer have an agent. As I have mentioned, agents tend to last about as long as policies. A loyal policyholder who doggedly continues with his contract until death will go through numerous agents. These orphans are scrutinized regularly by existing agents. The manager gets first choice, senior agents are next. Customers that look like they can be resold additional insurance are quickly claimed like a rich goldfield. Those who are advanced in years and with little income are pushed aside. Why waste time and effort on yesterday's customer?

I was intrigued by the statistics on a policy card for Mr. Callaghan. He was in his eighties and had faithfully paid $30 a year for over thirty years. The policy had been paid up since he was 65. He should have been a legend, held up as a shining example of all that is good and honourable in keeping faithful to your agreement. He had kept the policy until it was paid in full. He had the option of taking a portion in cash or keeping the insurance in force and paying no further premiums. An agent had seen Mr. Callaghan when the policy reached the paid up stage. There had been some talk about rolling it over into a larger policy—with more premiums and commission. Mr. Callaghan had declined. He was determined to see the original policy through to the end. No further contact was made with Mr. Callaghan.

Mr. Callaghan lived just a few miles from me. I decided to pay him a visit. I introduced myself and we talked over a coffee. He had been a farmer—no—he was still a farmer. He had never stopped. He had long since turned the farm over to his son, but he lived in the original farmhouse. His son had built a new Cape Cod next door. I asked him if he had ever had trouble making the payments on his insurance policy. He reminisced about the early years, with a young family and poor crops. He had been a potato and turnip farmer. He would haul his crop to town in the fall and sell it to a dealer. With the year's proceeds in his pocket, Mr. Callaghan made the rounds, settling accounts. First stop was to Scales Brothers for the seed and fertilizer. Then to Johnson's for the fuel and White's for the sugar and coffee and other household supplies that couldn't be grown. There was the payment for the potato digger and equipment repairs. Finally the insurance company got their piece. In the early years, turnips brought 40 cents a bushel. That translated into 75 bushels for one year's insurance premium. But he was determined to protect his family. The death benefit was $1,000— not a kings ransom, but enough to clear the farm debt. He longed for the time when the policy was paid in full. He was going to cash it in and take his wife on a vacation. They'd go to Florida; maybe stop and see some relatives in Boston on the way.

Mr. Callaghan never cashed in the policy. He never took his wife to Florida. She died when he was 62. There was no longer any need for the insurance. There was no need for the cash value of the policy.

Mr. Callaghan had retrieved his policy from his private papers. A lifetime stored in a small tin box. He was inquisitive as to today's value of the policy. The company's record that I had brought along gave the stark answer—$920. Mr. Callaghan looked pleased. I was embarrassed. I asked Mr. Callaghan: "How much are you getting for a bushel of turnips today?"

"Oh, about $11 a bushel."

I drove home thinking about Mr. Callaghan. Tucking aside 75 bushels of turnips in the early years. Every year. He had struggled, but succeeded. He had kept his side of the bargain, and the insurance company had held up their end. But it didn't seem equal. Over the years he had traded hundreds of bushels of turnips for this policy. Today the policy was valued at $920. That's only 84 bushels of turnips.

7

FINANCIAL PLANNERS:
WHO ARE THESE PEOPLE?

"Never trust the advice of a man
in difficulty." — Aesop

Many personal financial books give advice on how to
choose a qualified financial planner. This is founded on the
premise that such a person is essential to our future financial
well-being. If, indeed, this assumption is true, how do we begin
our search for such an individual? I once worked with a true
financial planner. He was a chartered accountant who went
back to school in mid-life and got a law degree specializing in
tax. His fees were substantial, but they were explained at the
beginning and there were no surprises. He could give advice
without bias for he was selling nothing but his knowledge. The
client got his money's worth. For the purpose of our
discussion, this is not the type of individual that we generally
encounter. For the most part, financial planners have stumbled

into their occupation by accident. In light of this we need to be selective in choosing who we will trust with our financial health. I maintain that the selection can be narrowed down to asking the likely candidates for one criteria and choosing based on the results of that piece of information. It does not involve listing education or designations.

Psychologists have long recognized the value of designations. Employees can be motivated by a title as often as with money. Give a person the position of supervisor and they forget that they haven't received a raise. A concierge is favoured above a janitor even though one cleans washrooms as well as the other. Companies hand out `Employee of the Month' awards, and universities and countries give honourary degrees to citizens. These designations all have merit. They are great morale boosters. They say, "Look at me. I have been recognized by someone." In some cases, designations signal a degree of expertise or education that gives an individual qualifications to perform a skilled task. This is helpful when we are looking for a doctor, dentist or vet. When it comes to financial planners ask yourself: What is the purpose of the training that merited the designation? Is it to provide better and more knowledgeable service, or is it to sell more product?

A few weeks after I began selling life insurance, I went to my first Life Underwriters meeting. This is an association of life insurance agents and their sponsoring companies. The goal is to advance the image of the insurance industry to the public and lobby governments for favourable conditions to sell their products. The association has brought pressure to bear upon politicians when they sought to tax certain aspects of life policies. They fought long and hard against the Canada Pension Plan. They perceived it to be a threat to their business of setting up savings plans for their customers. To this day, the insurance industry degrades the benefits of the CPP; telling individuals that it cannot be relied upon for their future retirement.

A further function of the Life Underwriters Association was to conduct a study course which when successfully completed entitled the agent to tack on a CLU after his name. I was interested to observe the recommendations of these agents. After studying courses on taxation and investing, would they sell a superior product than the rookie? The answer was no. They just sold more of it. I had long discussions with CLUs and would-be CLUs about the pros and cons of whole-life insurance. My conclusion was that there was a lot of pros trying to con a lot more clients. Their reasons for selling permanent insurance were wide and varied. Whenever there was a truly creative reason presented, the Life Underwriters newsletter would circulate it to encourage the troops. The one I remember was: "Whole-life insurance is the best policy for my clients because I can't make enough money selling term insurance. My clients need me in the business, and so whole-life is the best policy for them."

This staunch defending of a overpriced product was not just the view of a few life insurance agents who had CLU designations. It was the official position of the association. Once a year, the top producers in Life Underwriters received recognition for their efforts. In tallying score, term insurance was frowned upon. For a $100,000 permanent insurance policy, you were awarded 100,000 points. For a $100,000 term insurance policy you received 15,000 points. Indeed, many of the marketing managers who were responsible for high-commission-low-return products were graduates of the CLU program. I respectfully declined to join Life Underwriters.

In the late 80's the mutual fund industry was booming. The public was becoming more aware of stock market activity. Many were disenchanted with the life insurance industry as an instrument for savings. The refrain, "Buy term and invest the difference" was finally reaching a chorus so loud that even the life insurance companies could no longer ignore it. Within a few years you could hear the CLUs singing the words as their new anthem. Of course like so many Rice-Christians there was a reason for their conversion. The insurance companies scrambled to introduce their mutual funds and merge them with insurance policies. Had whole-life insurance disappeared? Only the name. To this day there is a reluctance on the part of insurance agents to look at life insurance as an expense that is temporary in nature and can be eliminated when the need for financial protection is over. They continue to promote a blending of insurance protection with a savings element. You may not hear the name 'whole-life,' but you may hear 'universal-life.' There was also a need to rename the agents. It was time to become Certified Financial Planners (CFP). Candidates came from the insurance and mutual fund companies and, to a lesser extent, the stock brokers and banks.

Now that you know some background of the industry of financial planners it is helpful to meet some individuals. In the office where I worked, there were a dozen salesmen. If you are of the opinion that you need a personal financial planner, which of the following candidates would you select? Bill was a door-to-door salesman selling household items when he was recruited to sell insurance. Ted had been in real estate. When that market slowed down, he jumped into selling life insurance. Stan had sold vacuum cleaners. Dan was a farm equipment salesman and started to sell life insurance while he waited for better times in the farming community. He did so well that he stayed. Gerry had lost his job with the government, and George had been working in a department store. I had just sold a small business and was looking for a change. If none of these seem like individuals that merit your confidence, perhaps I could introduce you to a wider selection.

In April of 1981, the above agents were invited to a conference in The Virgin Islands as a reward for sales excellence. We joined about two hundred fellow agents and spouses as guests of the insurance company at an all-inclusive resort. The company spared no expense. Why should they? It wasn't their money. It belonged to the policyholders.

I questioned many of the other attendees about their career choices that led them to becoming the cream of the sales-force for the company. I discovered that our small selection was representative of the company as a whole. There were school teachers who didn't like teaching, building contractors who had gone bankrupt, even politicians who had lost their seats. We had chosen to be financial planners after being less than successful at a previous pursuit. Our manager had summed it up by saying, "If you pass the provincial exams and your body is still warm, you're hired."

My experience after I migrated into the mutual fund industry was the same. I am not renouncing the need for financial planning. Nor should you dismiss all those who are employed in this field. Many are hard-working and do a first-class job. But you should be aware of their background. I have never met a financial planner who dreamed of being one when they were in highschool. Have you ever heard children playing 'financial planner'?

OK, enough said. So what is the question that you need to ask a financial planner before he comes to work for you. If he wants to sell you a life insurance policy ask, "Will you show me all the policies that you have on your life?" The amount and type of insurance that a person carries will tell you much about how he truly thinks about the product that he is selling. Don't forget to ask, "Are these policies still in force?" Some agents carried their personal policies with them as sales tools. Unfortunately, they may have been canceled. If the planner wants to invest your money for you ask, "Will you show me your last three years' statements or tax returns so that I can evaluate your personal investment returns?" You may think this is too personal, but think. This person wants you to trust them with your future! The best test of one's investment savvy is the way he/she manages his/her own money. You need an honest relationship with your planner. She will know every detail of your financial picture, and it's only reasonable that you should see her expertise before you sign. How serious would you listen to your doctor telling you to stop using tobacco if she couldn't quit smoking? Would you go to a restaurant if you knew the cook was being treated for food poisoning?

You may discover that you can become your own financial planner. After all, who cares more about your future than you do? And with little money to invest and less and less insurance to buy, what financial planner will want to waste his time with your low-income state when there are bigger fish to fry?

8

TAXES:
A NICE SOURCE
OF INCOME

"You have the right to every
benefit allowed under the
law." Revenue Canada

I'm always short of quarters when I go to Victoria. Upon arriving downtown, I begin my search for a parking spot with a meter standing guard. It's not easy to find one. Oh, there are some parking spots, but not to my liking. I'm looking for a particular meter. It needs some time left on the clock. And so I begin my slow patrol, quickly joined by other like minded visitors to the area. Like an adult version of musical chairs: "Around and round the block we go, where I stop nobody knows." We carefully pass each spot with it's occupant and meter, eyeing both, looking for signs of life in one and movement in the other. Someone sitting in a car is enough to make the procession come to a halt. I wait patiently. Is she going to vacate the premises with time left on the meter, or is she just waiting for a passenger? A motor running is not a clear indication; but the glow of back-up lights sends my heart racing. Usually by my third circum-navigation around the block I have secured moorage at a meter indicating free parking. It is only after disembarking that you can assess your acquired asset. It never ceases to amaze me that the most frequent time left remaining is four minutes—a savings of 8 cents. I never bother to compute the cost of the gas I have consumed in my quest for this savings.

A dilemma occurs when there is 25 minutes remaining. Generally I need the full 60 minutes of time allowed on the meter. An hour's time costs $1.25. I have two quarters and a loonie. Do I squander the loonie for the needed 35 minutes, or slide in the 50 cents and try to be back before "expired" appears, signaling the meter reader who has already been alerted that I am in town? I put in the 50 cents, and return in 55 minutes in time to see the commissionaire slide a ticket under my wiper and walk away. I'm sure that's the mayor giving him a "high-five". I don't try to fight—no protests of innocence or pathetic drivel about why I was delayed. Free parking means you take what you qualify for, but you play fair. I drive over to city hall to pay the $7.50 fine, but first I need to look for a parking spot with a meter that signals free parking.

"Dummy," I hear you say, "use the parking garage."

Sure, you can find space in a parking garage. But there's no opportunity for free parking. Even worse, your pass is issued as you enter the building. The clock is running. You then must maneuver your way up and through level after level looking for an unreserved spot. By the time you park your vehicle and make your way down twelve flights of stairs to the street you have accounted for the first twenty minutes on your parking stub.

But I digress. On the rare occasion that I arrive at my destination and find a meter with ample time remaining to complete my business, I am ecstatic. It matters not what transpires from then on. I can have my mouth frozen and two front teeth extracted and I'll still be smiling. I can be interrogated mercilessly by an auditor from Revenue Canada and end the episode by thanking him. There is just something altogether marvelous about free parking. I have received an unexpected gift. Oh, I've hoped for it—even waited and jockeyed position for it. But, nevertheless, when it appears, it is unexpected. What is more, there is no denying it's value. It can be calculated on the spot.

My emotions are stirred in a similar manner on two particular occasions each year. One is when the budget is read. The Federal Budget sets the policy for government spending in the upcoming year.

In our adulterated version of Monopoly, we throw any tax money accumulated into the centre of the board. Taxes paid by landing on income tax, luxury tax or drawing a notice of house assessment or hospital tax are gathered to be won by the player landing on Free Parking.

Is not life similar? Governments do not create wealth. You

don't need to have a financial planner to know that. However, neither do they destroy wealth— they merely redistribute it, spilling a little along the way. Indeed it has long been suspected that Robin Hood was a parable invented by a politician to define his role in society.

We are in a game where the aggressive empire builders continually run the risk of taxation, whereas the low income players can seek out the opportunity to gather windfall tax dollars. How should this knowledge affect the way you approach the game? It causes me to think about landing on Free Parking whenever possible.

"Wait just a minute. Aren't low income people always complaining? Isn't this the group that the opposition parties claim to champion, demanding that the government alleviate their plight?"

Let me begin by asking, "Who's not complaining?" But consider this. Last week, the middle of January, much of western Canada was snowed in. This doesn't happen in Victoria but we still listen to others with a sympathetic ear. Schools were closed; most businesses let their employees go home early when the snow began; they remained closed the following day. The few offices that dared open their doors, had calls from employees lamenting about not being able to find their cars in the snow and regretting their absence from work. Teachers and students united in supporting the school-board trustees' wise decision to close the schools, preventing certain carnage on the roads. Fifteen minutes later the ski hills opened to a brisk business. Somehow the employee has located his car and driven by his office on the way to Whistler. And the teachers and students have found a safe route up the side of a mountain where ice and snow abound.

The difference is choice. When we want to engage in some activity we always find a way and enjoy it. But don't try and force us into doing something or being somewhere without our consent. No one wants to be held back when ambition burns in their very being as they clamour to climb the ladder to reach the middle class. Choosing to stay off the ladder with your feet planted firmly in low income is quite a different story. A story that can indeed end happily ever after.

Now can we get back to the object of our affection, the Federal Budget? The government has basked in the warmth of economic good times complete with budget surpluses and international praise. But like anyone who stays too long in sunlight, they have, on occasion, looked a little red in the face. They have become sensitive to the cry, from opposition Members of Parliament, of: "surplus on the backs of the poor," and "over a million needy children— a national disgrace." I love it. It can lead to only one thing. The budget will have to address these concerns. It's only a matter of 'how much.'

Don't misunderstand me. My heart goes out to the poor. Like all normal people, when I witness scenes of intense poverty, especially affecting the young and innocent, it is gutwrenching. But when I hear politicians chanting some slogan written by a policy advisor making 100 grand a year, I am not so inclined to feel the need to shed tears. The poor of North America are, for the most part, a different lot than from those of our less fortunate neighbours. Tell someone in Ethiopia or Bangladesh that their family is poor because they only make $22,000 per year. There are some very poor families and individuals in Canada, worthy of our help. However, to create some arbitrary dollar threshold and suggest that every family living below that threshold is disadvantaged and that their children go to school hungry is a sham and minimizes the condition of those truly in need.

For those choosing to live a simple, uncluttered life, the windfalls contained in many budgets can be like finding a parking meter with 60 minutes available for use. Sometimes the Federal and Provincial Governments behave like estranged parents locked in a custody battle. The result is double time. Let me list some of my favourites:

CHILD TAX CREDIT — When I was growing up my mom got $6 a month for my care from the government. I think it went to $8 for my teenage years. Every family got the same amount—even the Cummings who everyone knew had plenty of money. I suspect they used this gift from the government as a further deposit in the credit union for their child's higher education. My mom bought food, and once a year, I got new runners. For my daughter still going to school, my wife gets $145 every month. The province, not wanting to loose our affection to the wealthy parent in Ottawa, adds another $105.

Unlike when I was young, this gift is not handed out indiscriminately. It is reserved for the low income families. I'm happy to qualify. I'm thinking of having more children. It's tax free money and the working conditions are good.

GST REBATE — When the conservative government (remember them) introduced the goods and services tax, they paid heavily at the polls. Feeling the wrath of their supporters, a provision was made to return some of this tax to those "who could least afford it". That's another way to say low income and I caught a scent of more tax free money coming my way. When the dust had settled, the additional income for my family is $125 every three months. Sorry... not available for those above the poverty-line. Oh well, that's their choice. I think of my mother whenever I get my GST refund cheque. She gets one too (about $50) and I know she loves it. Several years ago when visiting my mother she revealed to me that she had taken up a new hobby. Someone had told her that people have a way of hiding money in the most unlikely places. One is in their cigarette packages. The trouble is they forget about it and often discard the savings away with their package. My mother had started picking up packages that she found discarded on the sidewalk. This posed a problem. My mother hates cigarettes as much as I do, and she shuddered at the thought of being seen picking up the remains of someone's addiction. She would have been horrified to have anyone speculate that 'here was another senior down and out looking for a cheap nicotine fix'. There was also the problem of what to do with the package once it had been searched through for valuables. It couldn't just be thrown back down. Littering runs contrary to my mother's personality. The packages would have to be stored in her handbag until they could be properly disposed of. By the time my wife and I arrived for our visit, Mom had her new vocation down to a routine. She would walk by a discarded package and when the coast was clear, turn and quickly swoop down on the unsuspecting booty. She would rifle through the contents like a pro. Failing to find anything but a match cover and phone number, the whole lot would be thrust into her purse. It was a piece of art—poetry in motion. Finally It happened. During our visit she struck pay dirt. I don't recall ever seeing my mother dance as lively or squeal with such delight. It was only $5 but it was free. No strings, no obligations, no taxes—absolutely free. We went out for lunch, her treat, and blew the whole bundle. She talked about this windfall for months, and the same gleam would be in her eyes with each recounting of the adventure. To this day she has a hard time walking past a disowned cigarette package.

Everyone should be able to experience that 'rush'. The feeling you get with such a gift. It must be the feeling a party loyalist gets when appointed to the senate. All of us have from time to time put on an old suit and discovered a five or ten in the pocket. That's nice, but it was always ours. You may think the same about the GST refund. Wasn't it mine in the first place? No, I bought something and legally paid the correct tax as prescribed by the authorities. The government, acting out of their Robin Hood syndrome, gave me a gift. Of course it didn't hurt to have someone label me as 'low income'.

The province, no doubt seeing my gratitude to the feds, gives me a $100 sales tax rebate for my family when I file my tax return. My return is filed with a thank-you card attached.

There is talk under way of further enhancements to our social fabric which I await with anticipation. In December 2000, inebriated from another election victory, our government promised a $250. grant to help with the higher cost of petroleum products. Of course middle income earners need not apply. As I write, the province has rumoured, but not guaranteed, some competitive gift. I'll be surprised if they risk offending me by not offering at least a token. I like to think it's coming from the taxes of the guy who wrote the speech for the Member of Parliament calling for aid for low income Canadians.

The province is even more indulgent to we the underprivileged. Medicare premiums for a family is $72 per month but for the low income the cost is reduced or waived completely. There are additional benefits, such as free chiropractor and physiotherapy treatments, as well as eye examinations. Under the healthy kids program for low-income families, children receive free dental and a hefty payment towards eye glasses. At the other end of the age spectrum, low- income seniors receive a subsidy if their rent goes above a specific percentage of their income. Of course, in British Columbia all local seniors ride the ferries free during weekdays and receive free prescription drugs after paying the dispensing fee. There is also a substantial tax rebate for owner-occupied homes. Here again seniors receive a bigger grant. I will not be surprised to see all of these programs tied to income in the future.

"Why don't you just go on social assistance and be done with it?" Did I hear someone ask that? Social assistance (or welfare) implies that I am not able to care for the basic needs of my family. I am not only able, but happy, to care for these needs and to assist those in need in the community. I just do not choose to pay much of my earnings into income tax. I'd rather work less and spend more time with other activities that I assign as a higher priority. As a result, I fall into a low-income category and qualify for many benefits not afforded to higher income earners. I do not set the income guidelines, but I am happy to benefit from these generous provisions. My family would still maintain the same standard of living without any of these programs. We have in the past. The function of any sound financial plan is to lessen your tax burden where possible. Many would like to pay no taxes and receive some of the benefits that I have outlined but are reluctant to slow down their spending habits. To my knowledge, this is an either/or situation. You cannot do both. Some try by hiding income or evading sales taxes with some form of underground economy. I find this distasteful. It is also foolish. When you offer to pay cash for a product or service to induce the other party to avoid putting this transaction on his books, you are in effect saying:

"I'm dishonest and can't be trusted. I am willing to lie and cheat the government. What about you?" If the other party agrees, all you have established is that there is someone else with your set of standards. How good will the warranty on his products or service be? I never liked playing Monopoly with a cheater.

The other time of the year that excites me is tax-filing. While others file their returns with a sense of foreboding and despair at the amount they have paid or owe (or both), I relish the exercise of preparing my return. It is the journal of last year's financial endeavours. It is the blueprint of the coming year's gifts, grants and rebates. Except for the two years I worked for the Royal Bank (just after giving up on graduation), I have always been self-employed. At times I have received T4 slips, but they are those issued by companies that I have controlled. We have all heard of the advantages at tax time of the expenses related to the self-employed. Many, of course, are exaggerated (or down right fictitious), but there are examples that stimulate one's imagination. When I sold insurance as a broker for various insurance companies, it always intrigued me that their selling seminars would be in Florida or the Caribbean during the winter season. A training seminar was a legitimate expense, somewhat like a fact-finding mission to a foreign country that ministers of the crown go on. It may be necessary to travel to a foreign country to study the spending habits of the rich and famous for my next book.

If you own a corporation, you might take a page out of Air

Canada's financial plan. One of the most valuable assets they bought with the purchase of Canadian Airlines was at the bottom of the Balance Sheet. Canadian had been running in the red for years and had accumulated a serious deficit. This was transferred with the purchase and you can be sure that Air Canada will make good use of this, offsetting any income they have in future years. Sears found the deficit that Eatons built up, prior to its demise, too good to pass up. You may find a similar match for your corporation. But do your due diligence and know all the liabilities and pitfalls involved.

Let's look at our friend from Chapter 3, Adam Rairrie. Adam's initial response to the burden of income tax was predicable. His focus was on getting ahead and making more money. The solution to his problem seemed to be to make more money. To pay the tax he would just "sell a couple more suits, a few more pairs of Gucci.". Of course he quickly learned that the beauty of our progressive tax system is: the more you make, the more you pay. Indeed, Adam was over-whelmed at the fact that his tax bill was increasing faster than his income. When his wife, Nancy, rejoined the working masses, it just got worse. I wonder how many working couples with children actually sit down and calculate the cost of both parents working? Perhaps they have, but like the Rairries, they feel they have no choice, even though her income really added very little to the family coffers. No this is not a sexist remark. It is offered, not as a directive for a woman to stay home, but that a couple may chose for only one parent to be earning an income. Feel free to substitute the opposite gender.

Slowly, over time, and with the reappearance of Raymond, Adam grasped that the only sure and reasonable way to reduce his income tax was to lower his income. Ironically, by making this decision, he solved other financial and family problems. This is true Free Parking thinking. Adam stepped away from the vortex of: work...pay tax....more work.....more tax. He took time to methodically think matters through to their logical and satisfying conclusion. Will Adam and Walter, along with their wives continue to flourish as they get older? Of course. You can follow them with their retirement program in chapter 9. But first, consider the tax plan that Adam constructed for his family after he left Barton Brothers.

Adam chose window cleaning as a business for a number of reasons. He was familiar with the work and knew he could not only do it, but do it well. The start-up costs were very small. This is sometimes a draw-back, since many competitors are able to go into business overnight. Adam correctly assumed that he could earn a modest living. His customers found him to be reliable and fairly priced. Since he had no employees, his customers knew that his standards would be consistent. Many of Adam's customers were small businesses and homeowners who paid as soon as the work was completed. Adam had cash in his pocket the first day he was in business. This was important in the early months of Adam's new work.

Nancy worked from time-to-time with Adam. She would answer phone calls and arrange appointments. For the first few years, Adam paid Nancy $500 a year for her help. Since Nancy was able to earn this amount without triggering any tax implications, it became tax-free in Nancy's hands. Their daughter, Sarah, was also involved in the business. As early as age 11, Sarah would join her Dad after school. She was great at carrying some of the small squeegees and all the householders loved to visit with her. It was no accident that Adam always got his best tips when Sarah was along. Naturally, Sarah was compensated for her efforts. The first year, Adam paid her $1,000. By the time she was 18, Sarah, who was now an accomplished window washer, was earning $6,000 working part-time alongside her dad. All tax-free income. Until Sarah left home, her income was included in family income and was added when rebates and such were determined. However, it rarely had a negative effect since the total family income was kept at a modest level. Adam kept a close eye on the qualifying cut-off for these government programs. If the family was in danger of earning too much, he would schedule a holiday. His customers understood.

How many years have you heard the tired refrain? "The tax burden of the country is being carried on the backs of the middle class." Well, I don't know about you, but when I hear someone (usually a opposition politician) say that, I immediately think: "if this is true, then I certainly won't choose to be in the middle class." This leaves two other classes, upper and lower. People are a little squeamish about classes so they are referred to as upper-income and lower-income earners. Sit down here with me on Free Parking and think into which of these two groups would you seek admit-tance? I'll give you some numbers to help with your decision. We begin with 1000 graduates, all wanting to be upper-income. Of these, 100 will reach their goal. They will pay plenty of taxes. In addition they will pay lawyers, accountants and personal managers their ever increasing fees as they play hide and seek with Revenue Canada. Their advisors will become upper-income or middle-income earners, with tax burdens of their own. In the wealthier provinces, in good times, a further 600 will make it into the middle-class. We already know why we don't want to join this fraternity. Not only do they pay too much tax, but they are generally miserable. Their conversations vary between: "Do you know how much tax I pay?" and "If I could only get a break, I'd be in the upper-class". I have a feeling that this class will swell in size in the near future. As the business community comes to terms with the implosion of many high-tech companies, those who were comfortably seated in their upper-income leather arm-chairs, may find themselves struggling to pay their way in middle-class. They will spend their severance pay on divorce lawyers and psychiatrists.

Our group of 1000 will include, on average, about 300 lower-income earners. Many will struggle with their lot in life and fail to enjoy what they do have. Some will recognize what is their's and enjoy life to the fullest. One thing is guaranteed. The lower-income earners pay little tax. Yet they still spend money on many of the things that the upper-income earners buy. For example, Statistics Canada says that the average family earning $15,000 to $20,000 a year will still spent $733 a year on alcohol and tobacco. That's almost one-half of what a family earning $130,000 spends on these items. These low-income earners also spent an average of $931 a year for recreation. Despite the common perception, it appears that low-income earners do have a life, along with some discretionary spending. Of course these are only averages. Families that are prudent and judicious with their resources can prosper under the poverty-line.

Let's recap. The government, the keepers of the purse, proclaims that every man, woman, and child over the age of 16 shall dutifully declare all monies earned. It is then determined, what each person should be able to earn without interference, a basic exemption from the eyes of those assigned to squeeze the blood out of us 'turnips'. Everything above this basic exemption is fair game. You can defer income, transfer income, even create expenses to nullify income, but all of this will be examined if it is above the basic exemption. Your taxable income is calculated and then, according to a further determination, you are required to pay. Your money is put in the centre of the board along with millions of other like-minded citizens. Some of it comes from the consumer tax, GST. Even if you believe the story about all the millionaires avoiding income tax you should believe this. The GST is indiscriminate, if you buy to consume, you will pay. The doctor, taking home $200,000 will find a way to spend most of that money. If he spends it in Canada, much of it will attract the GST.

Our government wastes some of this money. There are

overpaid bureaucrats, shady politicians, and inept officials that siphon off millions of tax-payers' dollars. But, in reality, this is a small fraction of what is gathered. Their efficiency (or lack of it) is comparable to many big businesses and better than many charities. Take an optimist viewpoint. Do not fret about what is lost. Focus on what is available. The mandate, of the ruling party, is to distribute this wealth that they have garnered from the rich. It is their quest to travel throughout this great land in search of the "poor" in order to bestow upon us this wealth and relieve us of our miserable existence. With a little planning, you can qualify. Picture in your mind's eye all that money, sitting in the centre of a colossal Monopoly board. Your goal is to advance to Free Parking. Go ahead, you can do it! Taxation need not instill fear; with proper financial planning, it can be a ready source of income.

9

RETIREMENT
PLEASE:
AND HOLD THE TAXES

"I advise you to go on living
solely to enrage those who are
paying your annuities." — Voltaire

Many years ago, when I was selling life insurance, London
Life ran an ad about the virtues of permanent insurance.
Viewers watched in envy as a middle-aged couple escape the
typical Canadian winter. The couple had bought a policy that
provided them with the protection when they needed it, and
now, at age 55, they are living off the proceeds of their wise
investment. London Life, to my recollection, had no policy
named Freedom 55. Nevertheless, the ad was a success. To
this day, I can still see the tanned bodies of the happy couple
enjoying early retirement. Of course, this is advertising; and we
all know that it bears little resemblance to the truth. Some of
the insurance agents who worked for this company may have

found their retirement on the beach by now, but I doubt that anyone who bought the permanent insurance that was being promoted has met with the same fate. Yet, who could resist the lure of early retirement with the wherewithal to travel to tropical exotic places, free from the anxiety of the nine-to-five life.

Climb up on your Free Parking space and look at retirement. What do you anticipate your retirement will be like? Seriously. Do you want some help in looking ahead? Look around you. Your parents or grandparents, your elderly neighbours, what is their retirement like?

"But my retirement will be better because I'll have enough money to do all the things that I've been putting off. Things that I didn't do because I couldn't afford it or didn't have the time with my job and the kids to care for."

Look again. All the seniors that you see around town, why aren't they sitting on a beach in Bali or Hawaii? No money? I don't think that's the main reason. Most of the seniors that I know, by the time they get to 75, are happier to stay close to home. At that age, you begin to sense your mortality and there are too many concerns about health and safety when traveling abroad. Then again, you may be the intrepid adventurer at age 75 but what about your mate? If you plan to start retirement at age 60, you may have 10 to 15 years before you, too, decide that home is the best place to be. If you're convinced that you will spend these years traveling, you need to prepare now. Those who are serious travelers have honed their craft with years of practice. Most have taken extended vacations throughout their working life, rehearsing for the future. But how do you finance a great vacation on a low income?

A few years ago, my wife and I spent two weeks in Mazatlan. We had such a good time that we went back two years later with two of our children. Our initial trip cost under $1500. I think we could have done it for $1,000. Let me share a few thoughts on vacations and life. Contrary to popular belief, the measure of 'a good time' while vacationing is not directly proportional to the amount of money you spend.

If you arrive at Mazatlan Airport and a friendly Mexican (they are all friendly) offers you a free taxi ride to your hotel, listen to his proposition. He probably wants to sign you up for a timeshare presentation. In Mexico, these people approach-ing you are known as OPCs, roughly translated as "other people's cash". They are true entrepreneurs. Lately there's been some disturbing media reports about timeshare selling pressure tactics, but I speak only from our experience. The OPCs were always polite and took rejection graciously. The salesmen, who were usually Canadians or Americans, were pushy but knew when to concede defeat. If you accept his offer of a "free ride", the OPC will accompany you to your hotel. He has invested a taxi ride in you and wants to verify where you are staying. If you haven't pre-booked a hotel, he is a good source of information on availability and pricing. However, just like back home, don't believe everything you are told. On the way to your hotel, he will tell you about the property and any incentives that you will receive for going to the time-share presentation. It usually includes breakfast and a gift certificate for about $40 for supper or tours. Can you imagine what a great dinner you can have in Mexico for $40 US? You can say no and pay the $20 taxi-ride or agree and be whisked off to your hotel. He'll be back in the morning to take you to the presentation. On the way to the property, the OPC will continue to pre-qualify you. He gets a commission for every couple he delivers and a bonus if you buy. Remember, you have no intention of buying. Buying is bad. I'll tell you why in a minute. I always tell the OPC that I will not buy. Usually they say, "No problem. The hotel just wants the opportunity to show you their property, and maybe you'll change your mind." Fair enough. If you're asked how much money you make, be honest. If they're looking for high or middle-income earners, this may disqualify you and you can go on with your day. You had a free ride to your hotel and met a local who will never forget you. On our second trip, I was standing at a bus stop when a young lady came up to me and called me by name. She introduced herself as the OPC who had taken me to a presentation two years before. Some of the locals had nicknamed me "big spender", a tribute to their sense of humour—or is that sarcasm?

More than likely, regardless of your economic status, you will be ushered into the presentation room. A few quick words will transpire between the OPC and the hostess and you are introduced to the first salesman.

Don't let the salesman's lack of appetite dissuade you from enjoying your breakfast. You may be his second or third customer. Each one comes with breakfast. Let him make his best presentation. You'll get the full tour of the rooms and facilities. When he begins to close the sale, you need to firmly decline. Thank him for the tour and breakfast and inquire as to where you pick up your gift certificate. If the salesman senses that there is any chance that you will buy, the process will continue. He will introduce you to another "closer". It may help if you remind him that you came on the offer of a tour of the property and for the gift certificate and not to buy.

On our first visit to Mazatlan we went to seven timeshare presentations. Besides being fed seven times, we received and made use of $200 worth of certificates for tours and dinners. We also received $50 cash. How else could you get paid to visit the best hotels and resorts in town? When we decided to return, we knew which resort had the rooms and facilities we wanted. Even though we didn't buy, that resort did benefit from the presentation when we returned. We ate in the restaurant and tipped the cleaning staff. But we didn't rent the room from the resort. They wanted $200 per day. We paid $40!

If you need any reminders as to the folly of buying a timeshare, you only need to look in the classifieds. Why are normally prudent consumers so eager to sell their timeshares that they just acquired? Look at the money that they are asking. Often it is less than half of what they paid a few months ago. What have they discovered after the purchase? It's not just the several thousand dollars that you need to plunk down for your designated suite. It's the ongoing annual fee. I'm sure that the fellow who dreamed up the timeshare business model must have been a former life insurance executive. I was immediately struck by the similarities. There is the emotional sell, the inflated price and the ongoing drain of your bank balance. You pay as much as the salesman thinks he can charge. Oh, there is a listed price, but it's there only to imply value. While we were at the sales presentations, we saw numerous people buying identical suites for the same time frame, but at different prices. At one session, in which I exhibited too much interest, the sales manager in a final attempt to close the deal, showed me the contract that he had just concluded with a couple at the next table. He offered me an identical room for the same weeks but at one-half the price. This offer only made me more convinced that what he was selling was not a deal at any price. All of the money from the sale can easily be given to the marketing team. The resort needs none of this money. Their money comes from the annual maintenance fee. This fee is set by the resort management and will escalate. When we returned two years later, at peak season, it was obvious that half of the suites were vacant. Nevertheless, the resort was happy. The suites had all been sold. For numerous reasons the owners were not able to use the suites. There is a provision to bank or trade weeks, but my inquiries have revealed that this is seldom done. If your plans change there is not enough time to reschedule. The majority of the time, the rooms remain vacant and the owner continues to pay the annual fee. Allowing for scheduled maintenance of two weeks per year, each suite had been sold the other 50 weeks. The resort was receiving a maintenance fee for each of these 50 weeks. Can you imagine the profit generated when the suites need no cleaning because they are empty?

How did we rent a $200 a day, two bedroom suite for $40? When we decide to return to Mazatlan we started looking in our local papers and on the internet. We had no trouble finding people who wanted to rent or sell us a suite in our chosen resort. We made a deal with a couple from Victoria to rent their suite for two weeks for $600 Cdn. Their annual maintenance fee was $800 US. It has since gone up. They have owned the suite for 8 years. During that time, they have used it once and traded to stay in another property once. Their purchase price of over $20,000 US has been a financial embarrassment. For us, it was a great vacation... and a lesson on living.

Always listen to someone with an idea; but don't be quick to buy in. Wait a few days. If it still sounds like a great deal after you've checked it out, you can still go back and buy. If the salesman tells you that this is a one-time offer and you won't be able to match it later, walk away. That's a sign that something is not right. Either there is something wrong with the product or the salesman is lying. Even if it's just the salesman's way of closing the deal, you don't want to buy from him. He has compromised his integrity. Remember, when buying items like timeshares in Mexico, you may waive the right to cancel the deal, after you've laid out your money.

For those of us sitting on Free Parking and observing life we can benefit from the experiences of the rest of the players. Liquidation companies thrive on poor decisions of others and you can too. You can buy items for a fraction of their original cost when the owner realizes the error of buying on impulse. Even when planning on buying, you may be wiser to rent first. Paying you to go to an open house is not the focus of the marketing company; but if the offer is there and you play by the rules it can be a profitable excursion while on vacation.

When we speak of vacations, it is usually assumed that it involves traveling long distances. If you go to the local airport you will observe that not all the vacationers are leaving to have a good time. Many have spent hundreds of dollars to come to where you are. Find out why and then join them. Hordes of tourists come to British Columbia every year. Americans, Europeans and Asians come to Victoria with cameras flashing. They charter boats and search for salmon. They hire guides and look for steelhead.   Some come to watch the migrating whales. Others are here for the skiing, golfing or sailing. This all takes place within 200 miles of my door. We've lived here for over 10 years and there are many areas next door that we have yet to explore.

At the local marinas lay million dollar yachts, visible testaments to wealth. Moored alongside are modest boats of all shapes and sizes. When you're sitting on deck with a good friend and a glass in your hand, the size and cost of the vessel is of little concern. We have enjoyed our 21 foot wooden sailboat as much as if it had been a 65 foot yacht. No, even more. If it was larger, we would have more maintenance. We would not be able to sail for the better part of the year using 10 gallons of fuel. We could not haul it home when we're done and moor it in our driveway. We couldn't lift the keel and beach it on a sheltered shore and explore away the warm afternoons. Can you put a price on spending a week silently gliding under the gentle hand of a favouring breeze? In the evenings you can pick one of countless coves to anchor for the night. You might cast a crab trap or try your hand at catching numerous species of groundfish. While you watch the night sky in all its splendour, uninhibited by city lights, it's hard to give serious consideration to advice that says you need more money to have a good time.

We don't all live near the Pacific, but I have been a tourist in every province in Canada and much of the States. There are wonderful, exciting things to do, wherever you call home; and, regardless of your financial status, that's where you will spend most of your retirement.

"Forget the traveling. I'm worried about having enough money at retirement to pay the rent." Yes, this is a real concern for those without company pension plans. But are these concerns well founded? The wisdom from financial advice columns is unequivocal. We need to systematically put aside money for our future. The sooner the better; the more the better. But once again what do the facts reveal? Follow me as I accompany Sandy and we witness:

The Tale of Two Grannies.

You'll remember Sandy and Tim from earlier chapters. Once a month, she takes the ferry to Horseshoe Bay and then catches a bus to Vancouver. She visits both of her grandmothers and returns the following day. Her grandmothers are both fairly active for their age, but that is where the similarities end.

Grandma Clarke is a widow. Her husband was a history teacher at a local highschool. He was a good provider and a prudent fellow. When he died suddenly six years ago at age 72, all his affairs were in order. The house had been in his family for two generations. Like the other family assets, it was in both of their names. It was an easy matter for Mrs. Clarke to acquire sole possession after his death. His teacher's pension entitled his wife to `survivor benefits' of 70% of his former salary. Canada Pension pays her 60% of his pension. In addition, Mr. Clarke had carefully set aside some of his salary for several years prior to retirement. With time, this nest egg grew until it is now $300,000. It sits quietly growing under the guise of GICs and Canada Savings Bonds. Mrs. Clarke's income from the pensions amounts to $55,000. Her son is content knowing that she has been well provided for and is comfortable in her retirement.

Grannie Moreau has been divorced for 24 years. After her divorce, she got a job at a local grocery store. She worked for low wages for 16 years until she retired. There was no company pension and never enough left from her cheque to begin an RRSP. Mrs. Moreau's only income is from Old Age Security and a small Canada Pension. Together with the Guaranteed Income Supplement she receives $1100 per month. Sandy worries whether her grandmother has enough to eat. She has decided to ask Grannie to come and live with them in Victoria. Sandy will spend the night at Mrs. Moreau's and talk about her idea. Therefore, she goes to Grandma Clarke's house first.

It takes a couple of transfers to at last get to her final bus stop and then there is a ten minute walk. There are few of the old houses left with their acre lots and long lanes in Vancouver's west end. Sandy has always loved visiting her grandparents. They had reserved a bedroom just for her for as long as she could remember, upstairs and down the hall to the left. The windows are framed in laced curtains. There is a huge canopy bed covered with stuffed animals that were added to each year. Now she spends a few moments lying on the bed surrounded by her childhood memories. Then it was downstairs to join Grandma Clarke for lunch.

"I'm thinking of selling the house." The words came from nowhere without emotion. They had been hidden between "How was the ferry ride?" and "More soup?".

"Oh Grandma, you can't sell your house! Why would you think of such a thing?"

"I can't afford to keep it." There. She had put her thoughts into words. The voice was higher now, her feelings could no longer be restrained.

"Can't afford it." Sandy slowly repeated, trying to grasp the meaning. Was there another meaning? Surely it was not 'afford' in the sense of money. Everyone knew about Grandma Clarke's money, the pensions, the savings. "Grandma, I don't get it. Why would you say that? What about all the money that you and Grandpa had?"

"I still have most of it, but not for long the way things are going. I loathe this time of year. I pay the government every three months and then in April, I have to pay more. It gets worse every year. It' not fair. I just got back from the accountant's office. Did I tell you that I have to take a taxi now? Twenty dollars! I spent $20 to go to his office so I could pay him $300 to send $20,000 to the government. I came home and checked my blood pressure. It goes up at this time of year. If Jack was here ..." Mrs. Clarke didn't continue. Jack wasn't here. He had been dead for years, and wishing him back wouldn't help.

Slowly as the afternoon passed, Sandy heard the full story. She had remembered correctly; her grandmother received $55,000 in pensions every year. Then came the expenses. Income tax assessed her $15,000 on her income and a further $5000 on the $15,000 interest she earned on her savings. Like many her age, Mrs. Clarke didn't like to touch her savings, especially to pay taxes. The interest continued to accrue, and so the full $20,000 came from her pensions. The other tax bill is courtesy of the city. Her home is more than a cherished possession. West Vancouver has become the desired location over the years, and the assessment reflects it. Once a year, she is faced with the prospect of paying $8,000 to stay in her home. Other house expenses grow with the age of the old place. Last year it was the plumbing. This year, the drive-way—and she doesn't even own a car. When Sandy added in the hydro and heating along with the yard maintenance, she was in shock. Mrs. Clarke was left with $16,000 for her personal care.

When her grandma broke her hip a year ago, Sandy had stayed with her for the first few weeks after she came home from the hospital. Then it was arranged for a lady to come in five times a week to help out. Sandy knew that there was a government program for care-givers. Grannie Moreau had used it when she was convalescing after her surgery. A care-worker came for 2 hours everyday and Grannie paid $6. It was great, but Grandma Clarke didn't qualify. She had too much income. Her care-giver cost $18 per hour for 15 hours a week.

The hip had healed but Mrs. Clarke couldn't walk as much now. It was too far to the bus stop. The taxis were there to take her when necessary, but she resented the price. As Sandy continue to add up the costs, she understood what her grandma had meant. She wasn't eating cat food, but what was hers to keep was less than the government's take-- and that just didn't seem fair. Sandy tried to convince her to use some of the savings. But the investments were destined for her heirs. She had been raised to live within your means. You don't spend more than you make. To use the savings would signal failure on her part. It would be easier to cut back on spending, even if it meant parting with her family home. Sandy saw her grandmother, no longer the matron of a fine home with a comfortable retirement, but an old lady victimized by possessions and income.

As the bus wound it's way through the streets of West Van, Sandy looked at the fine homes in a new light. How many held their masters captive? There was no rescue for Grandma Clarke. The government would not come to her aid. She and her late husband convinced Ottawa long ago that they could look after themselves. The government had responded by stripping them of the Old Age Security and increasing their portion of income tax. The province followed by withholding many of the social programs for seniors. They directed their efforts toward those in need—the low-income seniors.

Within minutes, the city put on a new face. Tudor houses gave way to nondescript storefronts with names that identified the various ethnic communities. The subdued regime of the upper class replaced by the helter-skelter clamour of multitudes in the throes of life. It was in this environment that Mrs. Moreau had immersed herself after her marriage had failed so long ago. She rented a two bedroom apartment three floors above a Greek restaurant. As Sandy stepped into the elevator she was greeted with the smell of lamb and garlic. Her stomach told her it was supper hour. She had lingered at Grandma Clarke's in an effort to help. If Grandma Clarke was feeling squeezed by her expenses, how was Grannie Moreau surviving?

"Hi Grannie, sorry I'm late. Grandma Clarke said to say hello. If you haven't started supper, why don't we go downstairs? My treat. Doesn't it smell great?"

"Sorry, too late. Supper's almost ready. I think it's my lamb you're smelling." And so it was. Roast rack of lamb with all the trimmings. Rice pilaf and squash, Greek salad, even a bottle of wine, it was all there.

"That was some feast, Grannie, but you really shouldn't. I can't imagine how you can afford it." It sounded like a question that needed a response and Mrs. Moreau was up for the challenge.

"Nonsense. I've never had it so good. I should have got old years ago." Her face was bright; her eyes danced as she spoke. There was no trace of fear or frustration that Sandy had seen in Grandma Clarke.

"Could you help me out here?"

"Sure. How much do you need?"

"No, it's not money!" Sandy blurted out and then saw the joke in her grandmother's face. Mrs. Moreau had long sensed the concerns of Sandy and her husband. She had even heard the rumors of her moving in with them. It was time to lay any concerns to rest, but you couldn't blame her for having a bit of fun. When the laughter subsided, Sandy resumed.

"I've just been talking with Grandma Clarke and I know she's struggling with all the expenses. I also know she gets a lot more than you do and so. . ."

"And so you thought I must be living on the street with nothing to eat?"

"Well. . .could you explain how you manage?"

For the second time that day Sandy went through the budget process. It was hard to believe that these two grandmothers lived less than five miles apart. Their finances reflected two different worlds. Grannie Moreau receives the Old Age Security and the Guaranteed Income Supplement that are denied the higher income Grandma Clarke. What is more, she pays no income tax. Whereas Mrs. Clarke needs an accountant to assist her to keep her taxes in check, Mrs. Moreau can complete her simple form in a matter of minutes. She has an incentive to file early. She receives a B.C. tax rebate of $50 for being in a low income bracket. With the income information from her tax return she qualifies for the GST rebate of $200 per year courtesy of the federal government. The province uses this same information to pay her medicare premiums.

Remember Mrs. Clarke's other large tax bill—property tax? Mrs. Moreau escapes this as well. She rents her housing and because of her low income the province chips in $150 every month for her rent. Like Mrs. Clarke, Mrs. Moreau doesn't have a car, but she isn't worried about taxi fares. She pays $60 per year for an unlimited bus pass. The bus stops outside her apartment building. She loves the bus rides downtown .You travel through Greece and Italy, then the Philippines and Vietnam. The communities swarm with life and she is happy to be a small part of it. Sandy discovers that Grannie Moreau has indeed more than enough to care for her needs. She even has some to give for charities and a little for savings. There's no vast investment account with its annual tax liability; no house to care for and fret over.

Sandy is reminded of their evening at the Sandersons', talking of careers and possessions. When the Sandersons talked about growing old and giving up their care-taking responsibilities they had talked with confidence about their future income. On their annual vacations they spent time with their children who were doing volunteer work in South America and Mexico. As long as their health permitted they would continue this routine. Their lifestyle sounded so simple and reasonable. Little did she realize that her old grannie had already been living that life.

10

ESTATE PLANNING:
A DYING BUSINESS

"Let's choose executors and talk
of wills: And yet not so, for what
can we bequeath save our deposed
bodies to the ground?" — Richard 11

I've been thinking... thinking about my dad. He died last year at the age of 78. He loved animals but wasn't that crazy about people. He was a hard worker but never got the hang of managing money. If he had a dollar he would spend it. This is only hearsay since I was never there when he actually had a dollar. I mean a dollar that really belonged to him, that hadn't recently been borrowed from a finance company or unsuspecting relative.

The last nine months of my dad's life were spent in a nursing home. I was always impressed by the wonderful care he received. The staff treated Dad like a millionaire, but of course he was far from it. But he wasn't far from real millionaires. On the same floor resided those who must have made their financial planners' hearts swell with pride. They had squirreled away every spare penny over the years. Even now they worried about overspending. That's what made them Dad's neighbours. Dad was in a government run, heavily subsidized facility because he didn't have the $135 per day for private care. Some of his neighbours were there because they couldn't bring themselves to pay the cost. Or maybe they felt that this was going to be the last chance at getting something back for their tax dollars. For these ones, after a long wait, they could spend the rest of their days paying only $55 per day and the government picked up the rest of the tab. I wonder if they knew that the guy in bed 18c was only paying $26.

The government does an ability-to-pay examination and they determined that my dad could only afford to pay the minimum— $26. They would know, since they were his only source of income. Remarkably, Dad, confined to a nursing home, was finally unable to spend all the government was giving him. I talked him into using his newfound riches to pay off some debts. Had he lived another year, I think he could have left this world about the same way he arrived, debt-free. Unfortunately, time ran out, and at his death his total assets amounted to a bank balance of $1324. Revenue Canada says he owes them $2200. I believe them. So you see, I've been thinking. If my dad, who never heard the phrase financial planning, could eat whenever and wherever he wanted, drink enough to cause his doctor concern, smoke enough to shorten his life expectancy and still end up almost even, what is all the fuss about? It appears that we are spending an inordinate amount of time and effort on planning and arranging our financial affairs. If the worst that can happen is that we die without leaving a sizeable estate, then I question the validity of the whole exercise. If on the other hand you could convince me that longevity or happiness is somehow related to financial planning, then you would have a most willing convert. I'm not suggesting that you use my dad as your mentor. But, have you started thinking?

The natural successor to Financial Planning is Estate Planning. Like the tax man, the financial planner hangs on to you, his customer, until death (or you run out of money). The goal of estate planning is to arrange your affairs in such a manner that upon your death the designated beneficiaries receive your generous gifts with ease. A primary focus is income tax. Revenue Canada remains in your life longer than you do. The government is content to wait. They have applauded your every financial success. You might say that they have more than a casual interest in your financial plan. If your spouse has predeceased you, upon your death there is no more deferral of taxes. It is time to find out, once and for all, if all that planning was of value. The record of estate planners is flawless. You would be hard pressed to find one of their customers who complained that their plan didn't work well after their death. It must be as credible as a life time warranty on a casket.

Can we take a minute or two and pick up the trail of our successful Mr. Jackson from chapter two? He and his wife had diligently worked and saved their way to being millionaires. He never really retired, but when he decided to slow down and enjoy the fruits of his labour, they spent a couple winters down south. Then his wife got sick and he cared for her lovingly for the next two years until her death. Following his wife's death, Mr. Jackson spent a year traveling but he no longer enjoyed it. He was alone. When he returned, he was still alone. Oh, he had friends at the club and business associates but their conversations always reminded him of his wife and the brevity of life. He spent his last few years close to the family home with all its memories. He spent time with his accountant, worrying about the taxes he was paying and would pay at his death. Ahead of him lurked not just the final income tax, but probate fees, additional lawyer fees and executor fees. All were prescribed at a percentage of his estate. The more he had, the greater the costs. He talked with his lawyer at great length as he tinkered with his will. It seemed inevitable that his son would receive the bulk of his estate. As the years had passed, young Carl had become more and more impatient. He was over fifty and had grown weary of waiting for the fortune that he had long since claimed by reason of birth. Mr. Jackson felt guilty. He had been too busy working and planning to play with the boy. He had thrived on the challenge of providing things for those he loved. He never noticed the other needs of his son until it was too late. His son would never have the joy of seeing the fruits of his labour; going to bed satisfied, knowing that he had provided for his family with his own sweat. He was disabled in the cruelest way possible. Most disabilities are apparent, or at least can be diagnosed. But young Carl's affliction was a tragic side-effect of prosperity. There was no medical terminology that would foster under-standing and compassion like "fetal millionaire syndrome". Even if he had somehow planted a seed of ambition, it would be pale and spindly, growing under the shadow of his father's legacy. In his later years, Mr. Jackson had read of the pattern that was appearing around the globe. It was the cycle of Rags to Riches and then Riches to Rags. It encompassed three generations and he could recognize the symptoms in his family. It was a worry that Mr. Jackson took with him to his grave.

What are the alternatives? Contemplate the final chapter in the lives of the Sandersons. There is no denying that they, too, will grow old and fall in death. Their final years may be glutted with sickness like so many. However, unlike many, they have not had to squeeze their golden retirement into a few fragile years. There are no regrets wishing that they had spent more time earning more money so that they could pay more taxes. They can face death knowing that they have a already passed down a wonderful inheritance to their children. They have been given the skills to care for themselves and others. They have seen in their parents an example of success; not by the measure of how much you can acquire, but by the happiness one experiences in the sheer joy of living and sharing.

Bequeath to your offspring fond memories and wholesome values, compassion and a sense of humour. Give them memories of warm carefree days spent together. Memories confirming that you valued them, far more than your house, mutual funds or RRSPs. There are no lawyers, accountants, taxes or fees associated with such wealth. What is more, such treasures do not diminish but rather multiply as you generously give to those you care about.

So what's it going to be? Listen to the "experts" and fret about how to make more money so you can max out your RRSP and other investments with the prospects of a few prosperous tax-paying years of retirement before you turn your estate over to your heirs and worry how they use it? Or. . .how about a game of Monopoly? I'll race you to Free Parking!

THE LAST WORD

Free Parking goes to press next week. It's been six months since I began the process known only to would-be-authors and their longsuffering immediate families. Several publishers are still waiting to get back to me. For me, the gestation period is coming to full term and I'll have to be my own midwife. Financial information is dated and for the charts on the Dow and Nikkei to be relevant, I have decided to push forward.

The NASDAQ high tech market is looking more and more like the Japanese market of the past sixteen years. It's off 60% from its highs and still gingerly feeling for a firm bottom. The mutual fund sales force has reacted predictably. There have been calls for calm in the face of doom. Some have been bold enough to suggest that it is business as usual and even daring enough to say that it's a good time to buy. This"good buy" call reminds me of the cynical comment about the stock market good buy recommendations. "Good bye savings!" Investors are writhing in anguish. Greed has been replaced with fear. Some have turned to the courts. I remain a passive observer, sitting on Free Parking.

Here in British Columbia, politicians are knocking on doors, with cap-in-hand, looking for work. All are promising less taxes and more money — for low income families. As was rumoured last fall, on the heels of Ottawa's energy rebate of $250 to low income families, the provincial government bellied up to the bar and handed over $100 in an insurance rebate and a further $200 energy rebate via B. C. Hydro. Last week I received another $100 from the province to assist low-income families faced with rising energy costs. What a country!

ABOUT THE AUTHOR

Alan Dickson has been a bank employee, janitor, restaurant owner, sign maker, window tinter, insurance and investment salesman. He is a recovering financial planner.

More importantly, for the past thirty years, he has been a full-time husband and father. In this capacity, he has met with varying degrees of success, but due to the large-heartedness of his family, his contract has been extended.

Alan is a seasoned public speaker and has conducted classes at community schools on insurance and investment topics. His contrarian views provoke lively discussions.

Alan lives with his wife Debra and daughter Emily in Duncan, British Columbia. If you would like additional copies of Free Parking or to speak with Alan, contact:

Preferred Marketing Inc.
870 Government Street
Duncan, B.C. V9L 1B6
(250) 748 -5661

Free Parking

ORDER FORM

Please send me ____ copies of *Free Parking* @ $19.95 ($14.95 U.S.) Plus $3.00 s/h. Orders of two or more copies are shipped free of charge.
Canadian residents add 7% GST

Name _____

Address_____

_____

_____

Phone #_____

E-mail _____

Please send cheque or money order to:

Preferred Marketing Inc.
870 Government St.
Duncan, B. C. V9L 1B6
www.freemoneypress.com